CRUCIBLE of the UNIVERSE

GENESIS

by Dr. Lester Sumrall

LESEA PUBLISHING
P.O. BOX 12
SOUTH BEND, INDIANA 46624

Biblical references are mainly from the King James Version. Those from the New International Version are used by permission from the publisher. Those from the Revised Standard Version are so designated.

Italics in Scripture references have been added by the author for emphasis.

In order to avoid confusion, all pronouns for deity are capitalized.

All Scripture referrences not otherwise designated are from the book of Genesis.

ISBN 0-937580-61-9

CRUCIBLE of the UNIVERSE

GENESIS

DEDICATED

to the

MEMORY

of

HOWARD CARTER

of London, England

My Mentor

My Teacher

My Traveling Companion Worldwide

and

My Best Friend

Contents

Introduction

History is the story of man.

Without man there is no history.

Genesis records the dynamic history of the human adventure.

Recently, the book of Genesis came alive to me when God exploded into my mind that its fifty chapters cover half the human experience. The events of this one book alone span almost 3,000 of man's allotted 6,000 years of mortal history: 2,000 years from Adam to the Flood (chapter 7), and 1,000 years from the Flood to the death of Joseph (chapter 50).

The rest of the human story comprises another 1,000 years from the death of Joseph to the birth of Jesus Christ, and a final 2,000 years of our mortal history from the birth of Christ until He returns to the earth to set up His Millennial Kingdom. At that time, God's immortal resurrected children - from all generations will reign with Him for a seventh period of 1,000 years.

Today the bookshelves and libraries of the world are labyrinths of ever-changing human wisdom and information, crammed into musty tomes shoulder-to-shoulder with slick chrome-coated paperbacks.

Man, trudging through this morass of confusion, cries, "How can I find the Way?"

"Where among these contradictions is Truth?"

"What is the purpose of Life?"

The answers are in Genesis.

The book of Genesis raises the curtain on Scene One of the drama of man's relationship with his world and his Creator. The setting is the exotic garden of luxury, called Eden. The action is the unveiling of the mortal and the divine. God is there, and God is a communicator. He invites man to become acquainted with Him, to experience His nature and strength, His care for His children, and His holy hatred for disorder and rebellion. He is revealed as Creator, Benefactor, Judge and Savior, Teacher and Friend.

People have more misunderstanding about God than anything else in heaven or on earth. The Hindus in India, for example, do homage to 306 million little so-called gods. Is anyone expected to know all the names and all the things these little gods are supposed to do? The Bible tells us that the gods of the heathen are evil spirits, demons, deceiving the people. They are not gods at all.

There is one God, great and mighty, Who created the heavens and the earth. He is the true God and the only living God in the universe. As God the Father, He walked with Adam in the Garden; as Jesus the Son, He was God Incarnate in Israel; as God the Holy Spirit, He now resides within the very heart of every Christian, guiding him into all truth.

With no comprehension of the short, concise book of Genesis, we are limited in our understanding about God, about man, about history and world conditions today, and about hope. "Never has so much been owed to so little."

Genesis reveals God through the expression of His power as the God of love. Not that God is power. He is the Source of all power, but He *is* love. Through the operation of his power, He created all things in order to express His love-nature, and we come to know Him through the power of that love.

"Herein is love, not that we loved God, but that He loved us, and sent His Son to be the propitiation for our sins"
(1 John 4:10).

Genesis reveals man and woman in innocence in the Garden, holy, created beings in a holy place. Genesis also reveals Satan, the "adversary," hating truth, especially at the place of its origin. Genesis, therefore, is a battlefield. Because man sins, he loses his position with God and his place in Eden. All this background unfolds in the first three chapters. Then, from chapter 4 of Genesis through the book of Revelation, the Bible reveals the redemptive provision of God to elevate fallen man to a position of restored peace and fellowship with God and His Church in the eternal New Jerusalem.

Genesis is not remote, vague and incomprehensible. It is not veiled and mysterious. It is lively and light, exposing ignorance and superstition, while at the same time laying the foundation of the Christian faith. All further revelation depends upon the validity of Genesis, which opens in Eden and closes in Egypt, with the mummified body of the patriarch Joseph in a coffin, awaiting deliverance to the Promised Land.

Death, waiting for life.

Let us examine this vibrant chronicle of our ancestors as we walk down the path of Genesis together.

Lester Sumrall
South Bend, Indiana

1

The Genesis Crucible

Daybreak

Genesis, the book of beginnings.

Genesis, perhaps the most provocative word spoken by human lips--frightening to the atheist, thrilling to the believer; attacked by evolutionists, accepted as canon by Christian, Arab and Jew alike; execrated by humanists, acclaimed by more scientists and news-reporters than ever before as world events unfold.

Genesis, perhaps the world's most controversial book, is the daybreak of divine revelation, opening with the voice of Elohim, the "God of Faithful Strength," calling into existence that which did not exist.

There is enough theology in the opening sentence of Genesis to fill the world with books.

In the beginning, God created the heavens and the earth. (1:1)

A modern philosopher might take 200 pages to get to that point. He'd first do much preliminary investigation, then write a lengthy introduction. But God thrusts the truth upon us like the irrevocable thrust of a two-edged sword.

"In the beginning, God created . . ."

The Hebrew word, "bara," which means to create something from nothing, is used four times in three verses of Genesis 1. In verse 1, God "bara" matter; in verse 25, living things; and in verse 27, man.

Yes, Genesis is the crucible from which the earth in chaos emerges as a cosmos, a boiling pot from which outflows every evil and every good--every sin and every sorrow, every hope and every joy.

Genesis announces the beginning of everything except God Himself. With Him, there is no beginning.

Birthplace Of Light And Order

Genesis is the birth canal of light and order through the Word of His power. An astronomer observed that "there are more stars in the heavens than there are grains of sand in all the seashores of the world. We look and we think we see a star, but through a telescope it becomes thousands of stars...behind those stars, more stars, and behind those back stars, more stars. It frightens us; there seems to be no end of the universe."* God created all the stars and He named them, but not even the most sophisticated of man's computers can record even their existence.

Genesis is the cradle of life--of the

vegetable kingdom, the animal kingdom and man. Much of the intrinsic truth of society is recorded for us only in Genesis, not only of the family, home and community, but also of cities, nations, governments and continents, of language, art, music and literature. Genesis dramatizes the truth of sin, sickness and death, and the promise of redemption and everlasting life through *"the Lamb slain from the foundation of the world"* (Revelation 13:8).

Chapter 1 recalls the beginning of all creation. Chapter 2 relates how God created man, then breathed His own breath (spirit) into him, *"and he became a living soul."* Chapter 3 reveals man's rebellious and disobedient heart, separating him from his Maker. And the rest of the Bible offers to man God's way back to Himself. From the start, it is the colossal story of God and man--dust, deity and destiny.

Who's Deceived?

There is no complete Bible without Genesis. It is not a Saturday book to be thrown out with the trash. To repudiate the truth of Genesis is to destroy the fiber of divine revelation. To deny the supernaturalism of Genesis is to reject the final supernaturalism of Revelation. If Genesis is not literally true, then those who taught from it, including the Apostle Paul and the Lord Jesus Christ Himself, were deceived. If Genesis is myth or allegory, we are without supernatural revelation from God.

Of the sixty-six books in the Bible (excluding the Apocrypha), the other sixty-five repeatedly refer to the book of Genesis as a source of authority. Not only is it the most oft-quoted book of the entire Bible, it records the adventures of more heroes of faith as listed in Hebrews 11 (Abel, Enoch, Noah, Abraham and Sarah, Isaac, Jacob and Joseph) than any other book.

Adam is mentioned throughout the Bible in three other books of the Old Testament and five of the New Testament; Noah appears in five other Old Testament books and five of the New; and Abraham, fifteen of the Old and eleven of the New.

The writers of the New Testament refer to about 200 events and quote 165 passages from the book of Genesis. Twenty-five of these references were cited by Jesus Himself.* Of the twenty-seven books of the New Testament, all but three--Philemon, 2 John and 3 John--contain references to Genesis, and of its fifty chapters, only seven are not quoted or cited in the New Testament.** More than half of the 200 New Testament references are to the first eleven chapters, sixty-three of them to the first three chapters, and fourteen to the

Flood in chapters 6-8.

The Big Bang!

Many scientists, not comprehending the supernatural, have fought its truths. Philosophers have stood to make statements against its veracity. Humanists, the disciples of materialism whose god is ego, reject the book of Genesis by limiting their store of knowledge to sensory input plus imagination. Cosmologists, blatantly insinuating their theories into our school textbooks as facts, explain away earth's creation by God with a Big Bang somewhere out there.

Bang! And out of an enormous explosion came life?

Even if I were not a religious man, I couldn't accept that! Explosions are dangerous. Explosions are destroyers. No explosion ever built a building or constructed a wall.

No. The dependable beauty of a lovely flower, of a blazing sunset or a tranquil forest grove never evolved from an explosion. But, what if that rolling reverberating sound were Jehovah's voice, proclaiming, "Let there be!" That I could accept--Almighty God, creating the heavens and the earth by the Word of His power.

Cosmic Mud

Evolutionists tremble before the word

Genesis, frantically asserting that some spark of life from cosmic mud conjoined with another somewhere out in space, and somehow they got planted on the earth where they started life. They want to believe that part of that life multiplied and grew and increased through billions of years to become a family of proud peacocks, and some other part became a pecan grove. Peacocks and pecans from cosmic mud!

No! It was Jehovah's voice saying, "Come forth!"

While Genesis reveals God in His creative glory and majesty, redeeming man from the destructive results of his own ways, philosophers try to understand the whys and wherefores of life by searching the recesses of the human mind. Natural scientists pan for the hidden treasure in the streams of the dying planet. Humanists seek for truth in the excesses of the flesh. Many of these same scientists, however, in their costly study, research and experimentation, are coming to realize that in the book of Genesis lie the answers to their questions. They are even now recognizing the power of the human voice to build and to destroy, to change lives and to change situations, to heal and to kill. How much more the voice of God! As every judge seeks established precedents, so these scientists are establishing precedents for the truth.

Spoken Power

In the beginning, God created the universe, not with His hands, but with His voice. He spoke it into being. Is it possible? The Bible says it is. Jesus spoke the word in one place and in another place a dying man was instantly healed. (Matthew 8:5-13) That is spoken power. He spoke to the sea, and the winds and the waves obeyed Him. (Matthew 8:23-27) That is spoken power. He commanded the demons to come out of the Gadarene and they came out. (Matthew 8:28-32) That is spoken power.

Mouths Of Two Or Three Witnesses

Louis Pasteur, the great 19th-century French scientist, demonstrated conclusively that living things come only from living things, and because of his discovery, he saved the silk and wine industries of France. Nothing always produces nothing. Zero equals zero, whether alone or in multiplied millions. Only life begets life, and the God we acknowledge is alive and the Source of all life.

Even the 19th-century English humanist-philosopher, Herbert Spencer, wrote that there are five necessary elements for creation: time, space, matter, force and motion.* All these elements are incorporated into the first two verses of Genesis 1.

"In the beginning (time), *God created the heavens* (space) *and the earth* (matter)...*and the spirit of God* (force) *moved* (motion)...

When I was a student at the University of Chicago, one of the professors stood before the class one day and declared that not one whole page of Darwin's theories could stand the scrutiny of that day's knowledge and wisdom, and that was quite a few years ago. Charles Darwin, according to Oswald J. Smith, Litt.D., being greatly distressed before his death, confessed to his Christian good friend, Lady Hope of Northfield, England, that as a "young man with unformed ideas...(he threw out queries and suggestions...(and) people made a religion of them."

Oppose The Tide

Scientists who reject Genesis as the record of historical truth may just as well say, "I oppose the tide." Disbelief does not alter truth. No human knowledge or wisdom or ability can deadlock Genesis. We are amateurs in knowledge and wisdom and ability. God is not an amateur.

Man destroys, but God creates.

Man changes his ideas, but God's truth never changes.

Man learns, but God knows.

Man changes his friends, but his only eternal security is a partnership with God.

No store of information nor any profound philosophy ever changed a human heart. God changes not only hearts but also lives. The basic truth about all of us is in Genesis--that man is separated from God, that man has a degenerate nature, and that man lives in a society that suffers the results of that nature. Somewhere within that suffering society we are born, we live and we die.

Dispensations

Everything we know about the history of man, past, present and future, has its own place in time which can be divided into seven dispensations. During each of these periods of history, God deals with man through special laws and decrees. They are the Dispensations of:

1. Innocence,
2. Conscience,
3. Human Government,
4. Promise,
5. Law,
6. Grace, and
7. the Kingdom.

The first four dispensations, those of Innocence, Conscience, Human Government and Promise, are concluded in the book of Genesis alone.

The Dispensation of Law spanned the time from the exodus of the Jews from Egypt, when God gave Moses the Ten Commandments, to the establishment of the Christian Church in Jerusalem on the Day of Pentecost.

The present Dispensation of Grace, also known as the Church Age, will continue until Jesus returns to the earth in the flesh to set up His Millenial Kingdom with headquarters in Jerusalem.

Many great events of history are told in the Genesis Crucible--man's rebellion against a holy God, his resultant suffering, and God's mercy and grace. Does history repeat itself? Genesis is the proof. Since Genesis, *"There is no new thing under the sun"* (Eccl. 1:9).

*Pg. 14; Source unknown.
*Pg. 16; From chapters 1,2,3,4,5,6,7,9,17,18,19,28 and 31 of Genesis.
**Pg. 16; Chapters 20,24,34,36,40,43 and 44.
*Pg. 19; Synthetic Philosophy, by Herbert Spencer, pub. 1860.

2

The Genesis Timetable

No Void Creation

Any dating of the early years of mankind is difficult, and ours is not intended to promote controversy. We will not quarrel with those who believe that there was a pre-historic race before Adam because the Bible does not specifically state whether there was or not. The original Hebrew, however, seems to suggest that *"the earth became without form and void"* (Gen. 1:2). Isaiah assures us that, *"...the Lord, who created the heavens, who formed the earth and made it...did not create it a chaos; he formed it to be inhabited"* (Isa. 45:18 RSV).

What happened? We don't know. It is possible that the earth was the headquarters of Lucifer, the anointed cherub in charge of God's throne, before his prideful arrogance possessed him to say, *"I will ascend to heaven; I will exalt my throne above the stars of God..."* (Isa. 14:13).

Ezekiel explains God's response to Lucifer's ambition.

"Thus says the Lord God, You were in Eden the garden of God...you were on the holy mountain of God; in the midst of the stones

of fire you walked. You were blameless in your ways from the day you were created, till iniquity was found in you... Your heart was proud (and) I cast you to the ground'' (Ez. 28:11-15,17 RSV).

Could this be the time in which the earth became formless and empty? It would seem so. However, we are primarily concerned here with inspiration, with what God *does* say, and with His dealings with mankind beginning with Adam.

We understand that the time period from when Adam and his Maker walked in harmony to the death of Joseph in Egypt is roughly 2,400 years, followed by a lapse of about 430 years (to the birth of Moses) during which God was silent. (Another period of 400 silent years occurs between the Old and New Testaments.)

Six Glorious Days

Eternity is God's mystery. But, in the beginning of the commodity called time, there stand six glorious days of creation.

"And God said, Let there be light...
and the evening and the morning
were the first day...

And God said, Let there be a firmament...
and the evening and the morning
were the second day.

And God said, Let the dry land appear...

*and let the earth bring forth grass, the herb...
and the fruit tree...and the evening and the
morning were the third day.*

*And God said, Let there be lights...
and the evening and the morning
were the fourth day.*

*And God said, Let the waters bring
forth...and fowl that may fly...
and the evening and the morning
were the fifth day.*

*And God said, Let the earth bring forth
the living creature...Let us make man
in our image... And the evening and the
morning were the sixth day.*

*And on the seventh day, God ended
His work...and He rested.*

*And the Lord God planted a garden
eastward in Eden; and there he put
the man..."* (1:3--2:2,15)

Innocence

In the first dispensation, the Age of Innocence, God placed the man into the luxurious Garden of Eden, to *"dress it and to
keep it"* (2:15). (See Figure 1, below.)

The length of time Adam and Eve lived in
Innocence, we don't know. We do know,
however, that Adam's rebellion against God's
word and warning was deliberate. The Apostle Paul asserts that, *"The woman, being
deceived, was (caught) in the transgression,
but Adam was **not** deceived"* (1 Tim. 2:14).

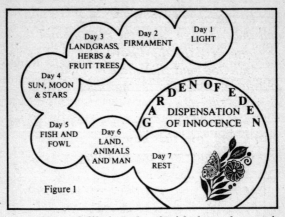

Figure 1

Adam deliberated, decided and acted, forging the way for humanity to say to God, "not Your will, but mine." And, just as Lucifer was discharged from his responsibility in the heavenlies because of his pride and willfulness toward God, so also the rebellious will of Adam is recorded as a warning of the consequences of willfulness in our own lives.

"All Scripture...is for instruction..." (2 Tim. 3:16).

God said, "What is this that thou hast done?" He pronounced a curse upon the serpent. He pronounced a curse upon the ground. He forecast sorrow for the woman, but He also promised that through her was the bloodline of redemption. She would produce the "Promised Seed," the Savior Who would destroy Lucifer, the "shining one" (who became Satan, the "adversary").

The Age of Innocence closes as Adam and Eve are banished from the Garden to live no longer in communion with Elohim, but according to the dictates of corrupt human conscience. Consequently, as Adam lived out his 930 years, he watched his children and his children's children seek and serve the world, the flesh and the devil.

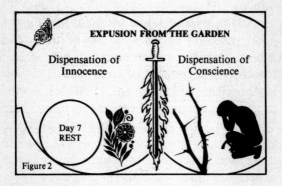

EXPUSION FROM THE GARDEN

Dispensation of Innocence

Dispensation of Conscience

Day 7 REST

Figure 2

Conscience

During the Age of Conscience, when every man did what was right in his own eyes, Adam's first son Cain became a murderer. What a price to pay for willfulness on Adam's part! Cain's victim, his brother Abel, knew God. He knew how to build an altar. He also knew that God ordained worship by a sacrifice-offering of blood in payment for sin. Cain proudly brought to God produce from his garden, the results of his own efforts. God refused him, but accepted Abel. Therefore,

Cain killed Abel, destroying the sacred bloodline at the same time. But God, in order to protect His promise, gave to Adam and Eve another righteous son whom they named Seth, through whom the promise would continue.

Adam had been banished from the Garden; Cain was further banished from the family.

Adam lived to know his great great great great grandson Enoch, who, according to the Bible, *"walked with God"* (Gen. 5:24). Enoch, a true prophet of God, named his son Methuselah, which means, "At his death, judgment comes." For 1656 years, the descendants of Adam, struggling with the knowledge of good and evil, would become more and more corrupt, until finally God would visit them with divine judgment.

"And God saw that the wickedness of man was great...and it grieved him at his heart.. And the Lord said, I will destroy man from the face of the earth, both man and beast and the creeping things and the fowls of the air; for it repenteth me that I have made them" (Gen. 6:5-7).

Little did Enoch realize that his son Methuselah's own grandson Noah would be the one by whom God would bring that judgment to the world, and that Methuselah, during the last 120 years of his life, would watch

Noah building an enormous boat far from any body of water.

Note the overlapping lifespans of these famous figures in Figure 3, below.

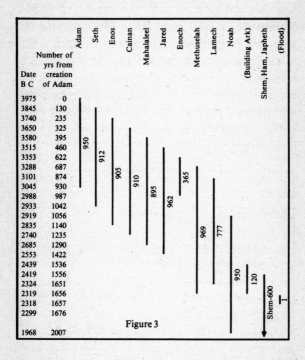

Figure 3

The fact that our forefathers of the Dispensation of Conscience lived hundreds of years longer than any since that time is possibly due to the protective propensities of the firmament waters, filtering the deadly space-rays before they hit the earth. Before the great Flood, there had been no rain from the sky.

God saw that the sinfulness of man would totally contaminate the world and the woman who was to give birth to the Promised Seed. Therefore, 2,000 years after His promise to Eve, He purged the contaminated earth with water, not primarily to destroy the world, but to save it. For Noah's uncontaminated family, God provided the Ark of Salvation to carry them through the Flood to a fresh new world. This time they would try human government.

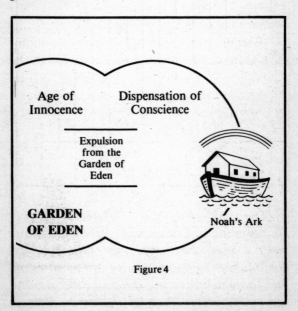

Age of Innocence **Dispensation of Conscience**

Expulsion from the Garden of Eden

GARDEN OF EDEN

Noah's Ark

Figure 4

Human Government

The Ark landed and, in obedience to the will of God, Noah and his family multiplied and replenished the earth. For 427 years the human race expanded, but the imagination of man was corrupt and the Dispensation of Human Government came to an end as the result of man's first serious attempt to formulate his own religion. He began to build the Tower of Babel, the "Gate of God." Here God makes the incredible observation:

"Behold, the people is one, and they have all one language; and this they begin to do, and now nothing will be restrained from them which they have imagined to do (Gen. 11:6).

Because of the evil and the power combined, God came down and confounded the languages of the people (11:7), divided their continents (10:25,32), and scattered them (11:8). Human government had failed.

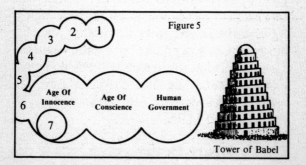

Figure 5

Age Of Innocence

Age Of Conscience

Human Government

Tower of Babel

Promise

From among the nations scattered throughout the world, God sought a man who had a heart for God, and He discovered an Eberite (Hebrew) in a city called Ur in the land of the Chaldeans, whose name was Abram and whose father was an idol-maker. Changing the man's name from Abram to Abraham, God called him away from his heathen inheritance and gave him a promise. He promised him that he would have a miracle-son named Isaac, and that through this son the Promised Seed would come to the world.

In contrast to the longevity of their antidiluvian forebears, Abraham died at "a good old age" of 175 years; Isaac died at 180; and Isaac's son Jacob the father of the Jewish nations, at 147.

Jacob, whom God renamed Israel, is the most often mentioned person in the Bible. His two names, Jacob and Israel, appear almost 3,000 times in one form or another. Jacob's eleventh son, Joseph, the last famous figure in Genesis, died at the age of 110. His body was embalmed and laid in a coffin in Egypt to await the deliverance of the Hebrew slaves to the Promised Land.

God's Heart-Desire

During the period from Genesis 1 through

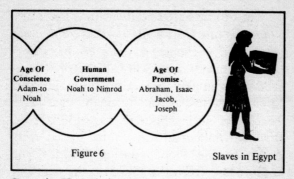

Age Of Conscience	Human Government	Age Of Promise	
Adam to Noah	Noah to Nimrod	Abraham, Isaac Jacob, Joseph	

Figure 6

Slaves in Egypt

Genesis 50 and the 430 years of God's silence from then to the birth of Moses, approximately 3,000 years, or one-half of man's allotted 6,000-year mortal history, unfolds. The generations from Adam to the Flood (BC 3975 to BC 2319) cover about 1,656 years; from the Flood to the call of Abraham (BC 2319 to BC 1792) 527 years; and from the call of Abraham to the death of Joseph (BC 1792 to BC 1606), 186 years.

Period	Dates	Years
Adam to Flood	BC 3975—2319	1,656
Flood to Abraham*	BC 2319—1792	527
Abraham to death of Joseph	BC 1792—1606	186
God's silence to the birth of Moses	BC 1606—1176	430
	Approx. total	2,799

Figure 7

The Apostle Peter tells us in 2 Peter 3:8, *"that one day is with the Lord as a thousand years, and a thousand years as one day."* For our purposes we will call the first thousand years Sunday, the second thousand years Monday, and so on through the week. Therefore, during Sunday and Monday, the first two millennial days, time passed from Adam to the Flood; during Tuesday and Wednesday, from the Flood to the death of Christ; and during Thursday and Friday, from the death of Christ to the present. We are coming to the end of the 6,000th year! We have come as far as Friday night! We are ready for God's Eternal Sabbath! For the Christian, the Eternal Sabbath is just the other side of death, the great Day of Christ when He shall reign as King of kings and Lord of lords.

God's heart-desire is to convert the sinning soul into a spiritual man, a son of God, a child of the King, a follower of Jesus, a joint-heir with the Son of God. Everything that happens on earth is to turn the people to Him that they might get to know Him, for to know Him as He is, is to love Him.

He offers the way of escape.

Jesus is the Way. He is the Right Road. (John 14:4)

He is Truth, personified. (John 14:4)

He is the Beginning and the Consummation of all things (Rev. 1:8), the Savior and the soon-coming King (Rev. 22:20).

Man once spoke a common language, and when the Lord Jesus Christ comes to rule on this earth, man will have a common language once again--one tongue, a pure tongue, a gift from God.

But first, judgment is on the horizon. Are you, like Noah and his family, prepared to escape the wrath of God coming to purge the earth, this time by fire?

*Pg. 33; In Genesis 11, in the line of Shem's descendants, "his son was born," by Hebrew usage is, more correctly, "there was born to him the ancestor of Shelah, and after that..." TLB.

3

Fifty Firsts

Introductions

Genesis, the crucible of the universe, is the book of introductions. More firsts rise to the surface of this seething cauldron of creation than of all other books combined, presenting a mysterious mixture of the glory and depravity of man. History down through the centuries from Genesis has proven time and again that *"...there is no new thing under the sun"*--no new joy, no new sorrow, no new sin, no new salvation, no new information, no new truth.

Modern society flipped the Bible to one side at man's altar to his new little god, Science, only to find that the new god vascillates and wavers, while the unchanging Word of God remains forever as fixed revelation and divine truth.

As Genesis opens, we meet the mighty Elohim, the one true and living God, as He initiates His plan for eternity. Then we are introduced to our world and the first of many things.

In the middle of the <u>first week</u>, comes the <u>first blessing.</u> God created the sea creatures and the fowls of the air, and He blessed them. (1:21,22)

At the end of the first week comes the <u>first holiday</u>, a day of rest.

"And God blessed the seventh day and sanctified it; because that in it He had rested from all his work which God created and made" (2:3).

The <u>first responsibility</u> given to man was by God Who placed Adam in the Garden of Eden *"to dress it and to keep it"* (2:15). Adam was the world's first horticulturalist, the <u>first farmer,</u> and he was to have dominion over all of creation.

Immediately after the creation of the <u>first man</u> and the <u>first woman</u> came the <u>first marriage</u> and the <u>first home</u> (chapters 1 & 2).

"Therefore shall a man leave his father and his mother, and shall cleave unto his wife; and they shall be one flesh" (2:24).

In the Gran Chaco Boreal, in the hinterland of Paraguay, I have watched primitive Indians in their marriage dance. The young unmarried men, with arms linked together, dance around a great bonfire, chanting, "Ho'a, ho'a, ho'a, ho'a, ho'a, ho'a, ho'a, ho'a," while each unmarried girl, sitting with the elders on the sidelines, decides which boy she wants to live with for the rest of her life. Eventually, she makes her choice, if she hadn't already, gets up and goes to him, takes his arm and dances with him. Thus, they are married before the tribe through dancing around the fire. When the fire begins to die, they go off together through the bush to create their own home.

In a great cathedral a costly ceremony performed with much pomp and show has the same purpose, to establish a home.

The Stage Is Set

In the first home came the deceiver with the first lie.

"Now the serpent was more subtil than any beast of the field which the Lord God had made. And he said unto the woman, "Yea, hath God said, Ye shall not eat of every tree of the garden? And the woman said unto the serpent, We may eat of the fruit of the trees of the garden: But of the fruit of the tree which is in the midst of the garden, God hath said, Ye shall not eat...lest ye die. And the serpent said...Ye shall not surely die..." (3:1-4).

...and the first sin, rebellion,...

"...she did eat, and gave also unto her husband with her, and he did eat" (3:6).

...followed by the first fear.

"Where are you, Adam? ...and he said, I heard Thy voice in the garden and I was afraid because I was naked and I hid myself" (3:10).

And so it is that transgression breeds fear. Today in our land there are more fearful people per capita than ever before in the history of mankind. Millions of people take all kinds of drugs to free them from fear: fear of the future, fear of death, fear of heights, fear of enclosure, fear of cats. They are crowding our hospitals, our asylums and our prisons because of their reactions to fear, and it all began with the first transgression.

Because of the first lie, God pronounced the <u>first curse</u> upon the serpent who allowed Satan to use him so effectively.

"And the Lord said unto the serpent, Because thou hast done this, thou art cursed above all cattle, and above every beast of the field; upon thy belly shalt thou go, and dust shalt thou eat all the days of thy life" (3:14).

The first curse was followed by the <u>first promise</u> of God and a prophecy to Eve that through her would come God's solution to their predicament, the Savior Who would conquer the enemy.

"I will put enmity between thee and the woman, and between thy seed and her seed; it shall bruise thy head, and thou shalt bruise his heel" (3:15).

This prophecy speaks of Jesus Christ, the Son of God, Who would come about 4,000 years later and bruise the head (a fatal wound) of the serpent, representing the devil, through His death on the cross (a temporary wound as the prelude to His resurrection).

More Firsts

Man's <u>first clothes</u> were aprons made of

dry, crumbly fig leaves, a ludicrous attempt by Adam and Eve to hide their shame. And on their behalf, God Himself performed the first sacrifice. He killed and skinned a lamb to make them a covering of skins. It was the first time blood was shed on man's account.

For centuries the Indians of Gran Chaco Boreal wore next to nothing--the men, tiny g-strings, and the women, slightly larger aprons. But, when they met Jesus and were converted, they were ashamed of their nakedness and asked for modest clothing.

The first angels to appear in the Bible are the mighty cherubim, guard-angels of heaven, at the entrance to the Garden of Eden to halt whoever might attempt to gain access to the tree of life.

"So he drove out the man; and he placed at the east of the Garden of Eden cherubim and a flaming sword...to keep the way of the tree of life" (3:24).

Angels appear throughout the Bible from Genesis through Revelation. I believe that in these last days there will be more angelic appearances to more people than ever before.

Adam and Eve's son Abel appears at the first altar, worshiping God with the sacrifice of an innocent lamb. His brother Cain brought an offering of the fruit of the ground, and the Bible says, *"The Lord had respect unto Abel and to his offering, but un-*

to Cain and to his offering he had not respect'' (4:4,5).

Thus was kindled man's <u>first jealousy,</u> his <u>first anger,</u> his <u>first hatred,</u> in the heart of Cain, culminating in the <u>first murder,</u> when he killed his brother Abel. The first man Adam's own son, a murderer!

"And God saw that the wickedness of man was great in the earth and every imagination of the thoughts of his heart was only evil continually" (6:5).

Cain's evil deed caused sorrow and sadness to his parents as they wept over the <u>first funeral,</u> and saw their son Cain become the <u>first fugitive.</u>

Glory And Depravity

God had put one man with one woman, but five generations down the line from Cain, Lamech was not satisfied, and Lamech practiced the <u>first recorded polygamy.</u> (4:19)

Lamech's son Jubal was the <u>first musician</u> (4:21) and Jubal's brother Tubal-cain was the <u>first craftsman</u> (4:22).

The <u>first-man-who-did-not-die</u> is Enoch (5:24).

A few generations after Enoch, the <u>first giants</u> appear. (6:4)

Noah's ark was not only the <u>first boat</u> (6:14,22), but also the biggest boat in history until 1850. He and his family lived aboard the ark during the <u>first rain,</u> which caused the

<u>first world-wide calamity</u>. (2:6; 6:17)

After the ark was grounded, the <u>first homosexual act</u> and the <u>first drunkenness</u> were recorded when Noah lay drunk in his tent and his youngest son Ham went in and abused him. (9:20-24).

Soon thereafter the <u>first political entities</u> --the first cities, nations and kingdoms--were established, the <u>first false religious cult</u> formed under Nimrod, and the <u>first zigurrat</u> built. (10,11:4,5)

When the <u>first famine</u> occurred, Abram *"went down into Egypt"* (12:10), after which he returned to Canaan as the <u>first general</u> and fought in the <u>first war</u>. (14) There he paid the <u>first tithes</u> to Melchisedek, the King of Salem (14:20) and was honored by God with the <u>first recorded vision</u>. (15:1)

The <u>first judgment on a city</u> was fire and brimstone rained by God upon Sodom and Gomorrah. (19:24)

The <u>first recorded dream</u> in the book of Genesis is that given to Abimelech, the King of Gerar, who had taken Abraham's wife Sarah into his harem.

"But God came to Abimelech in a dream by night, and said to him, Behold, thou art but a dead man, for the woman which thou hast taken; for she is a man's wife" (20:3).

The <u>first recorded love story</u> is in the book of Genesis.

"And Rebekah lifted up her eyes, and when she saw Isaac, she lighted off the camel. For she had said unto the servant, What man is this that walketh in the field to meet us? And the servant had said, It is my master; therefore she took a veil and covered herself. And the servant told Isaac all things that she had done. And Isaac brought her into his mother Sarah's tent, and took Rebekah, and she became his wife; and he loved her; and Isaac was comforted after his mother's death" (24:64-67).

In Genesis we read about the <u>first international betrayal</u> among the members of a family.

"Jacob went near unto Isaac his father; and he felt him and said, The voice is Jacob's voice, but the hands are the hands of Esau" (27:22).

The <u>first rape</u> was perpetrated upon Dinah, the daughter of Jacob, by Shechem, a prince who wanted to marry her. The <u>first reprisal</u> was because of this, when the sons of Jacob killed Shechem and his father, Hamor, and all the males of their kingdom, and returned Dinah to their father's house.

The sin of Tamar, was not only the <u>first adultery, but also the first incest</u>.

"And it was told Tamar, saying, behold, thy father-in-law goeth up to Timnath to shear his sheep. And she put her widow's

garments off from her, and covered her with a veil, and wrapped herself and sat in an open place, which is by the way to Timnath... When Judah saw her, he thought her to be an harlot; because she had covered her face. And he turned unto her by the way, and said, Go to, I pray thee, let me come in unto thee; for he knew not that she was his daughter-in-law ...and he came in unto her, and she conceived by him'' (38:13-18).

What Can Change The Human Heart?

Man, left to the sin and evil imagination of his own heart which tells him, "Don't bother with God; you'll get along all right," experiences broken hearts, broken homes and a broken society. He finds his loved ones in divorce courts, jails, insane asylums and hospitals. Sin is not new. It started in the book of Genesis, and it is rampant in your home town. The only answer is a change in the hearts where the trouble begins. Philosophy can't do it. Psychology can't do it. Education can't do it. Jails and prisons aren't doing it. The only power to change the human heart is the power of God.

Man needs a Savior. Man needs a Healer. Man needs to be in touch with his Creator. Man needs God.

4

The Big Week—Part I

Parallels

"In the beginning, God created the heaven and the earth. And the earth was without form and void; and darkness was upon the face of the deep. And the Spirit of God moved upon the face of the waters. And God said, Let there be light: and there was light. And God saw the light, that it was good: and God divided the light from the darkness. And God called the light Day, and the darkness he called Night. And the evening and the morning were the first day" (1:1-5).

As the thundering voice of Almighty God pierced the black opacity of space, light burst forth to repel and dispel the endless night. God divided the light and the darkness and they have never reunited. He separated them, and no power in the universe can blend them again.

It was the first day, and the Spirit of God moved. I believe that the days of creation were literal, actual days, and I believe that the movement of the Holy Spirit then was as mysterious and effectual in its power as His moving is today in the hearts of men, in homes and in communities, wherever men allow Him to move. As, when the Spirit of God moves in nature, things begin to happen, so, when the Spirit of God moves in a life, things begin to happen.

The first seven days of Genesis precisely parallel the progression of the spiritual life of a Christian.

Each of God's days of creation begins in the black shadows which must fade before a rising sun. The same is true in the spirit.

Day One. God's first day parallels the spiritual rebirth when His light upon the lost soul dispels the spiritual darkness in that soul.

Day Two. The dividing of the waters by a firmament parallels the Christian's separation from sin and his consecration to God.

Day Three. The generation of the plant kingdom parallels the bearing of supernatural fruit, love and joy and peace, in the daily walk of separation.

Day Four. God's setting of lights in the heavens parallels the Christian's witness to the world, resulting in the winning of souls to the Lord.

Day Five. The creation of the water and air creatures that adapted so readily to the elements parallels the victorious and overcoming life.

Day Six. The creation of land creatures and man, with his ordained dominion over all, parallels the Christian's reigning with Christ on the earth and eventually throughout eternity.

Day Seven. God's day of rest parallels the Christian's eternal holiday with God.

Day One—Light

In order to deal with spiritual darkness in hearts today, God works the same work as He did in nature 6,000 years ago. First He sends light to diffuse throughout both darkened world and darkened soul. And, as the first light that shined on the world revealed not order but chaos, so the first light to shine on the soul reveals not beauty but sin and death. The initial spiritual wonder in a human life does not happen through baptism or joining a church or some other ritual. The onset of holy spiritual phenomena in a life is the wooing of that soul to God by the Holy Spirit's speaking to the heart, convicting of sin and drawing that soul to the altar of confession, forgiveness and cleansing by the blood of Jesus shed at Calvary. Then the surrender of that life to God brings about the spiritual rebirth of the "new creature in Christ."

This is spiritual creation—not a reformed life, not a patch-job, but a brand-new creation. God speaks, and there it is. Then He takes empty hands and empty hearts and fills them.

When God says, "Let there be light,"

there is light. When He says, "Let there be prosperity," there is prosperity. When He says, "Let there be health," there is health. When He speaks, it is as He says.

The voice that told the darkness to go and the light to come is the same voice that speaks to hearts today. And, as the Spirit of God brooded over creation that first day, so He broods today over His spiritual children, driving away fear and phobia, guilt and superstition, while comforting them, caressing them and caring for their needs. The light of His Word, banishing sin, fear and confusion, brings forgiveness and understanding--a new day, a new life, a new experience.

"In the beginning was the Word...in him was life; and the life was the light of men" (John 1:1,4).

"For God, who commanded the light to shine out of darkness, hath shined in our hearts to give the light of the knowledge of the glory of God in the face of Jesus Christ" (2 Cor. 4:6).

Through Jesus Christ, the Logos (the Living Word) of God, we can be filled with that light. When one little light on earth switches on, all of heaven rejoices.

Jesus said, *"Ye are the light of the world."* The only spiritual light the world has is God's children. If our lights go out, the world is in darkness.

"God saw the light, that it was good" (1:4).

"Ye are all the children of light, and the children of the day; we are not of the night, nor of darkness" (1 Thess. 5:5).

God divided the light from the darkness, thereby establishing their boundaries. Light and darkness no more dwell together spiritually than they do physically. Nor do Jesus Christ and Satan share the same house. Pure water and bitter water don't come out of the same faucet. When light comes into a room, the darkness disappears. Light also drives out darkness in the human heart. No demon can hold out against the light, no evil influence can hold out, no power of unbelief can hold out, no bad habit can hold out against the light.

Day Two --Separation

"And God said, Let there be a firmament in the midst of the waters, and let it divide the waters from the waters. And God made the firmament, and divided the waters which were under the firmament from the waters which were above the firmament; and it was so. And God called the firmament Heaven. And the evening and the morning were the second day" (1:6-8).

Day Two speaks of separation and consecration--separation from sin and consecration to God.

The waters of the sky and sea were one with the land, but God divided the things of earth from the things of heaven, then separated them one group from the other. In the Christian life, the time of salvation is the time of separation from the things of the earth and consecration to the things of heaven.

"Be ye not unequally yoked together with unbelievers: for what fellowship hath righteousness with unrighteousness? And what communion hath light with darkness? And what concord hath Christ with Belial? or what part hath he that believeth with an infidel?...Wherefore...be ye separate, saith the Lord" (2 Cor. 6:14,15,17).

God is the great separator. We are separated from lying; we're separated from cheating; we're separated from evil speaking; we're separated from lust; we're separated from robbing and killing. He brings us out of chaos into cosmos, out of disorder into order and peace. It is the working of God in our hearts, not the will of man, not the will of the flesh nor the willpower of the human mind. God is equipping us for eternity. He is changing us. He is separating us from drudgery, from sorrow, from fear, from sin, from the practice of false religion.

The power is His. Our part is to receive it and use it, to trust and obey. Separation is a holy thing. When we try to live the separated holy life in our own strength, we're like the man who said, "I can stop smoking anytime I want to. I've already done it a thousand times."

Noah was a man who lived a consecrated life and, in the day of judgment, God separated him and his family from the world.

When judgment came to the twin towns of Sodom and Gomorrah, only Lot and his two daughters were delivered. When they turned their faces from sin, they became righteous in God's eyes and they were rescued from the fire and brimstone.

When judgment came to the Egyptians, the children of Israel were divinely protected from the plagues and pestilences. The frogs did not plague them, neither did the lice nor the flies nor the boils nor the fire nor the hailstones, neither did the locusts nor the darkness nor the death of the firstborn. They had kept themselves consecrated to God and separated from the sins of the Egyptians, from demon worship and infant sacrifice and immorality. Then, when plagues came, when sorrows came, when death came, they were set apart. The same God Who had separated them from the heathen in spiritual matters protected them supernaturally during the national disasters.

God will always preserve His children in time of judgment as He preserved Noah and

Lot and the children of Israel.

God's faithfulness to His children is displayed over and over, not only in Genesis but also throughout the entire Bible. The Word of God is true. The Word works. We don't have to set about to prove it. Our lives are His witnesses.

It Worked In Me

The Word worked in me. I was as mean as the devil until Jesus came into my life. First, He shined His light on my life to show me my dreadful condition. There was no beauty in it. There was no peace. It was chaos. The combination of sin and disease had just about wiped me out, but Jesus came into my heart, separated me from sin, took away the desire to sin, and healed my body which was in the final ravages of tuberculosis. The doctor gave me two hours to live, but Jesus healed me completely without any further medication.

Of all the young friends I had in Mississippi, Alabama and Florida in my youth, about two-thirds were dead before they were twenty-five years old. Of the few who are not dead, several are in prison.

My best buddy died before he reached twenty. One night, with a silk stocking pulled over his face, he was robbing the store owned by a friend of ours when the storeowner caught him in the act and shot him. Then, when our friend pulled back the stocking and saw who it was, he screamed, grabbed him up in his arms, pulled him out to his car and raced him to the hospital, blaring his horn and crying all the way. He was trying to save his life, but it was too late.

I could have gone the same way to the devil and to hell if it had not been for the mercy of God. I know Genesis is true when it shows God's intervention in the course of a life. I know it's real. I've got the seven days of creation right down through the center of my life. I am the living parallel of the great day when God said, *"Let there be light,"* and of the great day when God separated the light from the darkness. And my life reflects all the other days of creation as well.

I may never be very important, and I may never be called a great preacher. I may never stand very high in the estimation of man, but I am careful how I live. I want always to live the separated life. I don't want my example to cause anyone to be lost.

"It is impossible but that offences will come: but woe unto him, through whom they come! It were better for him that a millstone were hanged about his neck, and he cast into the sea, than that he should offend one of these little ones" (Luke 17:1,2).

God expects separation, godliness, holiness and purity in us. Sinners also expect it. Millions of people go to hell because of

professing Christians who do not live godly
lives. We will never bear healthy, wholesome,
spiritual fruit if our lives are unclean and im-
pure. God wants us to be different from the
world. Sinners are watching us, hoping to see
us make it, because we represent hope to
them. If we make it, maybe they can make it,
too.

*"All of creation waits with eager longing
for God to reveal his sons"* (Rom. 8:19) NIV).

5

The Big Week—Part II

Day Three - Fruit-Bearing

"And God said, Let the waters under the heaven be gathered together unto one place, and let the dry land appear; and it was so. And God called the dry land Earth; and the gathering together of the waters called he Seas; and God saw that it was good. And God said, Let the earth bring forth grass, the herb yielding seed; and the fruit tree yielding fruit after his kind, whose seed is in itself upon the earth; and it was so. ...and God saw that it was good. And the evening and the morning were the third day" (1:9-13).

On the third day, God commands the earth, "Bring forth!" Where before was lifeless desolation, grass and fruit and grain appear. The whole world was barren and forlorn, but God spoke. A tremor shot through the earth. Billions of tiny dead seeds trembled slightly, then cracked as life burst forth. Green blades shot upward toward the light as white thread-like roots burrowed through the soil in search of sustenance. The blowing gray dust became fields of swaying grain and orchards of blossoming fruit trees.

Life conquered death!

When God penetrates the human heart, the germ of eternal life takes root and spiritual fruit begin to blossom forth, the fruit of love and joy and peace.

"But the fruit of the Spirit is love, joy, peace, patience, kindness, goodness, faithfulness, gentleness and self-control" (Gal. 5:22,23 NIV).

God first sends the light to show us the way. He then separates us from the despair and confusion of the world, and a miracle begins to happen--supernatural love and joy and peace begin to flow from within. We don't manufacture the fruit of the Spirit. We are like trees that bear fruit because of life and power stored inside. It is love-power, joy-power, peace-power. Great changes occur in our lives, not as results of our own will; it is the power of God coming forth. It is God,

"...that is able to do exceeding abundantly above all that we ask or think, according to the power that worketh in us" (Eph. 3:20).

No dead tree bears fruit.

The life surging within the Lord Jesus Christ Himself, causing Him to rise from the dead, gloriously and eternally alive, is not temporal life. It is eternal life. He was not "rehabilitated;" he was "regenerated." In regeneration, the one who before produced only social dead works is now *"raised to walk in newness of life"* (Rom. 6:4), now equipped to bear spiritual fruit to the glory of God.

It was Jesus' physical body that came forth from the grave. The grave could not hold Him. His mortal body had become immortal; His corruptible body had become incorruptible. Where before His physical life was empowered by His mortal blood, it is now empowered by the Spirit. That is why the Apostle Paul says,

"...if the Spirit of him that raised up Jesus from the dead dwell in you, he that raised up Christ from the dead shall also quicken your mortal bodies by his Spirit that dwelleth in you" (Rom. 8:11).

Third day, "Bring Forth!"

Day Four --Witnessing

"And God said, Let there be lights in the firmament of the heaven to divide the day from the night; and let them be for signs, and for seasons, and for days and for years: And let them be for lights in the firmament of the heaven to give light upon the earth; and it was so. And God made two great lights, the greater light to rule the day, and the lesser light to rule the night: he made the stars also. ...and God saw that it was good. And the evening and the morning were the fourth day" (1:14-16,18,19).

The Word of God brings light to the understanding. The Word separates man from sin unto godliness. The Word brings forth the fruit of righteousness. The same Word that set lights in the heavens to rule the day and the night causes the Christian to be its witness to the world. The spiritual parallel, therefore, for the fourth day of creation is witnessing and winning souls to the Living Word, Jesus Christ, by means of the testimony of that same Word operating in our lives.

The sun here speaks of the Lord Jesus Christ, the "greater light." He is the Great Luminary, the "Light of the World" (John 8:12), the "Sun of Righteousness" (Mal. 4:2).

The moon, having no light of her own, represents the Church, reflecting light from the Son. If there is beauty in the Church, it's the beauty of Christ. If there is goodness in the Church, it is the goodness of Jesus. If there is glory in the Church, it is the glory of God in our Lord Jesus Christ, King of kings and Lord of lords.

"And they that be wise shall shine as the brightness of the firmament, and they that turn many to righteousness as the stars for ever and ever" (Dan. 12:3).

Notice the ministry of the lights--to rule by day and by night. Christians are the light of the world, the nation and the community.

"...the sons of God...in the midst of a crooked and perverse nation, among whom ye shine as lights in the world; Holding forth the

word of life..." (Phil. 2:15,16).

Life on this planet depends upon light. When light is excluded, life dies away. This is as true spiritually as it is naturally.

You no longer see what I was like when I was young. The darkness in my soul and spirit was killing my body. When the doctor gave me two hours to live, the light of God came into my life. The life of God pierced through my body and took residence, healing me and changing the direction of my life. That same light shines through my life today. I am a witness of God's power and presence among men. I am one of God's lights in the world. I could never have accomplished that in my own power. I did not heal myself from the ravages of TB. I did not save my own soul and bring life to my spirit. God did it. He saved me; He healed me. And He makes me a witness to others for Him, to sidetrack souls from the road to hell onto the road to life.

My Obligation

God's light reveals to me my obligation. I don't want to be like some Christians who sleep through the fourth day. When the light turns on, it's time to get out of bed. It's time to get up. It's time to get moving. It's time to follow the light.

I know when I'm being led by the light. For fifty years the inner light of God's love led me all over the world. I want to take a million souls to heaven with me, and God is leading me everywhere to find them.

When I was in South Bend, Indiana, God spoke to me one day and said, "Go to the Philippines."

In my heart I could see multitudes of people getting saved in the Philippines. Two years later, we held a revival in Manila which was attended daily for two weeks by 50,000 to 60,000 people. 150,000 of them made decisions for Christ. They experienced the light of God which penetrated the darkness in their souls and changed them. It separated them from the evil around them and they began to experience supernatural love, supernatural joy, supernatural peace and supernatural healings in their spirits, in their minds and in their bodies. Now many of these same people are witnesses and soulwinners throughout the world because of the power of God working in their lives.

Because God saves us, we have an obligation to get up. When He speaks, we have an obligation to obey. Because He loves everyone everywhere, we have an obligation to our neighbors. He wants them to know about Him, too.

Baby Christians are another type of spiritual fruit. Jesus said,

"Ye have not chosen me, but I have chosen you, and ordained you, that ye should

go and bring forth fruit, and that your fruit should remain" (John 15:16).

He is saying here that we can add to the Kingdom of Heaven by winning souls. Some of us will win *"an hundredfold, some sixty, some thirty"* (Matt. 13:23).

God does not favor barrenness. He told the man and the woman to be fruitful. He sent the animals and birds and fish forth to multiply. When we don't produce, something is amiss.

Is there light? Is there separation? Is there spiritual fruit? If so, there will be a harvest, not of oranges and pears, but of immortal souls.

"The harvest truly is plenteous, but the labourers are few; Pray ye therefore the Lord of the harvest, that he will send forth labourers into his harvest" (Matt. 9:37,38).

6

The Big Week—Part III

Day Five - Overcoming

"And God said, Let the waters bring forth abundantly the moving creature that hath life, and fowl that may fly above the earth in the open firmament of heaven...and God saw that it was good. And God blessed them, saying, Be fruitful, and multiply, and fill the waters in the seas, and let fowl multiply in the earth. And the evening and the morning were the fifth day" (1:20-23).

Life came to the earth in a surge of motion. By faith birds flew through the air, overcoming gravity. By faith fish and whales swam in the seas and did not sink to the bottom. They were overcomers, living victoriously the lives they were created to live.

The fifth day of creation illustrates the progressive Christian experience, the victorious life, the forward advancement into new experiences with faith to overcome.

"Who is he that overcometh the world, but he that believeth that Jesus is the Son of God. Ye are of God, little children, and have overcome...because greater is he that is in you than he that is in the world. And this is the victory that overcometh the world, even our

faith'' (1 John 5:5; 4:4; 5:4).

The cemetery is not the end of the road. The grave is not our final destination. God is equipping His people for eternity.

Jesus said, *"To him that overcometh will I grant to sit with me in my throne, even as I also overcame, and am set down with my Father in his throne"* (Rev. 3:21).

What is the purpose of it all? In the beginning, God created man in His own image and likeness, so compatible with Himself that He is able to live inside of man's body. He created him as an eternal companion for Himself that man might enjoy all of creation with Him forever. That compatibility has been marred. Either it must be restored in His creation or creation must be destroyed. The way of reconciliation for man was opened by the death of Jesus on the cross of Calvary. And those to whom it pertains are those who have accepted His righteousness in place of their own and are now "practicing" for eternity.

There is coming a day of universal shaking when all that is counterfeit, all that is pretentious, will fall away. Meanwhile, the testings and trials and temptations of the world, the flesh and the devil expose the unbelievers, doubters and rejectors of God, while at the same time confirm those who will inherit all things with God's Son.

"...Yet once, it is a little while, and I will shake the heavens, and the earth, and the sea, and the dry land; And I will shake all nations..." (Hag. 2:6,7).

"Multitudes, multitudes, in the valley of decision: for the day of the Lord is near in the valley of decision... The Lord also shall roar out of Zion, and utter his voice from Jerusalem; and the heavens and the earth shall shake; but the Lord will be the hope of his people..." (Joel 3:14,16).

"For the day of the Lord of hosts shall be upon everyone that is proud and lofty... And the loftiness of man shall be bowed down... and the Lord alone shall be exalted in that day.. And they shall go into the holes of the rocks and into the caves of the earth, for fear of the Lord, and for the glory of his majesty, when he ariseth to shake terribly the earth. The earth shall reel to and fro like a drunkard..." (Isa. 2:12,17,19; 24:20).

"See that ye refuse not him...that speaketh from heaven; Whose voice then shook the earth: but now he hath promised saying, Yet once more I shake not the earth only, but also heaven. And this word, Yet once more, signifieth the removing of those things that are shaken, of things that are made, that those things which cannot be shaken may remain. Wherefore, we receiving a kingdom which cannot be moved, let us

*have grace, whereby we may serve God accep-
tably...* (Heb. 12:25-28).

The overcomer can say, because of the
mercy and power and provision of God, *"I
shall not be moved!"* (Psalm 16:8).

Life in Christ begins at conversion with
victory over death and hell. It is sustained by
victories; it ends in victory. Jesus Christ is not
defeated. The Church is not defeated. The
sons of God are not defeated. The overcoming victorious life cannot be seen with the
natural eye for it is eternal, but the evidence
of it can be seen in the natural, as the fruit of
the Spirit colors the everyday walk of the
Christian on earth with the shades and hues of
heaven.

Christians are like the little dandelions.
When the grass grows three inches high, the
dandelions shove their heads up to four; if the
grass grows five inches tall, the dandelions
stretch to six. Tough little dandelions overcome their circumstances.

Day Six--Dominion

*"And God said, Let us make man in our
image, after our likeness: and let them have
dominion...over all the earth and over
every...thing...upon the earth...and it was so.
And God saw every thing that he had made,
and, behold, it was very good. And the evening and the morning were the sixth day"*
(1:26,30,31).

The sixth day of creation is the great day of dominion. No defeat, no backing up, no backing down. God says of the first, second, third, fourth and fifth days, that they were good. He says of the sixth day that it was very good. The path grows brighter and brighter, not darker and darker; stronger and stronger, not weaker and weaker; higher, not lower; gladder, not sadder, *"unto the perfect day"* (Prov. 4:18), the day we meet God face to face to live with Him forever, the day He says of our lives, "At the beginning it was good, but at the end it was very good."

From witnessing to overcoming to reigning with Christ, they flow together as in the days of creation. One prepares the way for the next.

God created man to be king of the earth, to have power and authority over it. He said to Adam, "Subdue it!".

How would you subdue a water buffalo that was lumbering down Main Street in your town? Would you stand behind a shatter-proof window of a store-front and shout, "Hey, Buffalo! Go home! Go home!" Hardly! You would take him by the horns, tie a rope around his neck, and show him who is master. That's subduing a water buffalo.

Man is to subdue the earth, not be subdued by it. God's power in us is sufficient.

Not Environment And Heredity

The sin of Adam repudiates the humanistic theory that the effects of environment and heredity control a man's life. Adam started at the top and he fell to the bottom. By an act of his will, he forfeited his personal relationship with God in the Garden of Eden through his own deliberate disobedience and lack of repentance. And he had no parents to blame--no evil heredity, no unfavorable home situation. He had no bad friends. He was perfect, created by a holy God. He had it made.

Man still chooses to sin. It's in his heart. Because of it, he lost dominion. The world is filled with defeated people. Man once had God's authority over all creation, but he relinquished it to satisfy the lust of the flesh. He changed masters from the God of Heaven to Satan, the *"god of this world"* (2 Cor. 4:4).

Jesus Christ, Who bore the curse of man's sin, is the only one who can restore man to fellowship with the Father. He wants to bring the whole human race back from second-class citizenship to the place of dominion.

The Last Adam

Through Christ, "the last Adam," we stand to gain more than the first Adam lost for us. The first Adam was merely innocent, a passive condition. Believers in Jesus Christ are made righteous, an active position before God. They are *"adopted sons"* (Gal. 4:5,6), *"seated with Christ in heavenly places"* (Eph. 2:6), and *"partakers of the divine nature"* (2 Pet. 1:4). We are capable of deeper joy than the unfallen spirits, who will never know the gladness accompanying salvation because they were never lost.

The Holy Spirit still broods over the earth, wooing man from his own affairs at home, at business, in prison and in jail, in recreation parks and ball fields, calling him back to God Who desires to restore the power and dominion he lost.

I Found It!

I have found the entrance to dominion with God. One day I noticed in my Bible study that Jesus did not pray for the sick to be healed. He simply commanded that they be healed. He had authority. He had dominion over sickness and disease. He simply said, "Come out!" and the infirm or unclean spirit obeyed and left the afflicted person. He said, "Be healed!" and the sick were healed.

And He said to His disciples and to us, "Do as I do!".

I used to pray and pray for sick people to get healed, but now I command them to be healed, in Jesus' name. I am the same person, but I have a different attitude. It came from reading the Word of God. I realized that it isn't Jesus Who puts sickness on people. It's the devil. So, I don't plead with Jesus to take it off. I command the devil to do it. And he knows by the tone of my voice that I'm not playing games with him. Since I discovered this truth in the Word, many times more people are healed through my ministry than ever before. I entered the sixth day and discovered spiritual reigning with Christ.

Day Seven

As God's days commenced with the shadows of evening, so the sunset of the glorious sixth day flowed smoothly into the seventh day of God's rest.

"Thus the heavens and the earth were finished, and all the host of them. And on the seventh day God ended his work which he had made; and he rested on the seventh day" (2:1).

God is relaxed. He perfected His creation in six days, and He is satisfied. He is not tired. He is not weary from the exertion. He has simply completed His project, created all His firsts, all His originals, and He is resting, looking it over and finding it very good. He is satisfied that His creation is worthy of Himself, manifesting His wisdom and His great strength. It is His domain. He is on the throne, but there is nothing more to add. Nothing will evolve into something better. He rejoices in the perfection, and will now govern, preserve and uphold the universe Himself.

God's seventh day was a special day, set apart. He called it the "sabbath." It is impossible to say just when it recurs for many reasons. First of all, the Bible does not specifically state that it ever ended. Then, too, when it's midnight in London, it's six o'clock in South Bend. And, since our calendar is different from the Hebrew calendar, that adds to the confusion. What we do know is that God rested on His seventh day.

The seventh day not only parallels our eternal rest with God but also the peace we have in the turmoil of this life. Christians are not like the restless sea, laboring back and forth. We have peace. We have tranquility. We have joy. We have rest in our spirits, knowing that we have an inheritance with God because of the Lord Jesus Christ.

God encourages us to set aside a special day to remember our Creator, to contemplate His works, to render Him our tribute and thankful praise, and to let Him know that we are glad of our relationship with Him.

Our rest in Him now in a world of unrest is a miracle. Jesus said, *"Come unto Me, all ye that labour, and are heavy laden, and I will give you rest"* (Matt. 11:28).

Rest is a commodity that millions of people are seeking through drugs, entertainment and sin. But God commands us to find our rest in Him, not to be part of a world of exhaustion and frayed nerves, but to relax in our salvation. Jesus said, "I will give it to you."

In my early life, before I accepted Christ as my personal Savior, I often wondered if I would ever find rest from worry. But for the past fifty years at home and abroad, I have rested in the knowledge that I am saved. And I know that my eternal rest is just on the other side. I'm not worried. I'm not anxious. I'm not afraid of failure or death or anything the devil can do to me. I'm safe in Jesus. I'm saved, and that is perfect rest. It's for all God's children, and it's for now.

Millennial Rest

We are looking forward to the millennial day of rest when throughout the world the mountains will no longer roar with guns. The earth will no more be overcome with pests and pestilence and perilous times. Sickness and sorrow will cease. No more death or separation; no more heartaches and tears; no more strife.

Since God's day begins with evening, right now we are counting down to the sunset of the sixth day which will usher in the day of eternal rest when we will be citizens of the eternal kingdom. Meanwhile:

On Mondays, pray for spiritual light.

On Tuesdays, pray for separation from sin

and consecration to God.

On Wednesdays, pray that you might bear spiritual fruit.

On Thursdays, pray for a chance to lead someone to Jesus.

On Fridays, pray for the overcoming life.

On Saturdays, pray for dominion.

On Sundays, praise God for eternal rest.

7

The Big Blunder

Adam, Don't Do It!

In the beginning, God created a 16,094,592,000-mile universe that is still expanding at 186,280 miles per second, the speed of light. Then He created man to rule beside Him and be His family throughout eternity. He made Adam in His own image and likeness, a spiritual immortal being, and He clothed him for a time in flesh made from the elements of the earth. Adam was a spiritual being in a physical body, empowered with the very breath of God--a living soul. God gave into the hands of Adam complete authority over all of creation, then placed him in the Garden of Eden, a perfect environment perhaps a thousand miles square.

"And the Lord God commanded the man, saying, Of every tree of the garden thou mayest freely eat: But of the tree of the knowledge of good and evil, thou shalt not eat of it: for in the day that thou eatest thereof thou shalt surely die. And the Lord God said, It is not good that the man should be alone...And the Lord God...made...a woman, and brought her unto the man...and they shall be one flesh" (2:16-18,22,24).

God endowed Adam not only with tremendous powers of wisdom and knowledge, but also with the privilege of choice and the task of naming all the animals on the face of the earth. What a mind he had! What abilities from God Himself! What responsiblity! The perfect environment, the perfect home, perfect peace, harmony, order, contentment and perfect happiness.

Into this perfect setting, clothed in snakeskin, came the ambitious Lucifer to do his dirty work. Possibly, he spoke sometimes directly with Adam; we have no information on that. But this time he sidled up to Eve. Even though Adam was present, somehow Lucifer cornered Eve in order to speak with her alone. That should have been a danger signal. He was dividing the family, and it's family unity that holds the human race together.

Lucifer tempted Eve through *"...the lust of the flesh* (body), *the lust of the eye* (soul), *and the pride of life"* (spirit) (1 John 2:16). He convinced her that the forbidden fruit from the tree in the midst of the Garden was *"good for food* (appealing to the flesh), *pleasant to the eyes* (appealing to the soulish imagination), *and to be desired to make one wise"* (appealing to spiritual pride) (3:6).

Rebellion Comparable To Witchcraft

Even though in God's eyes rebellion is

comparable to the sin of witchcraft, there it lay in the hearts of the first man and woman as it lies in the hearts of every man, woman and child today, to be tempted to rebel against God. It originated with Lucifer who said, *"I will... I will... I will"* (Isa. 14:13). In the Garden, he tempted Eve to exercise her own will against the expressed will of God. He tempted her through the flesh; he tempted her through the soul; he tempted her through the spirit. He won in all three areas. She never resisted. She never tried to stop him. She never called a family council. She tried to handle him in her own strength and wisdom, and she failed. She lost the battle. She was deceived. She invited Adam to follow her in the deception, and he did it.

Adam and Eve had been clothed from the beginning with the shekinah glory-fire of God, the non-consuming fire that was in the burning bush. (Ex. 3:2) When they sinned, they lost their clothing of fire. They lost the glory-covering of innocence, and they were naked. This is the most dreadful event in human history: the Big Blunder, the blunder of disobeying God, not receiving God's Word as the Truth, superseding God's authority, giving allegiance to a fallen angel, and forfeiting the garment of righteousness.

Our Unique Position

Adam and Eve had a unique position,

"made a little lower than God himself" ("Elohim," Psalm 8:5), with the power to choose their own destiny. We also have that unique position. We too can choose our fate. God will not force us to spend eternity with Him in heaven, and nobody can make us go to hell. It's our own choice. Nobody is in hell by accident.

When mankind died spiritually through Adam's sin, all of creation died with him. It is still in the death struggle, groaning and travailing because of the biggest blunder man ever made, the blunder of using the power of choice to choose against God's express will.

When Adam and Eve realized they were no longer swathed in glory, they became afraid and tried to hide.

God saw their terrible dilemma and with tender-hearted love, He called to Adam, "Where are you?"

This was Adam's chance. He could have repented, he could have confessed, he could have been forgiven. But again he blundered. He pointed his finger at the woman and in-directly blamed God Himself.

"The woman whom thou gavest to be with me, she gave me of the tree, and I did eat" (3:12).

The First Sacrifice For Sin

With compassion and sorrow in His heart,

God looked at the two standing before him, trying to disguise themselves with the dying leaves from a scraggly fruit tree. They had entered into the knowledge of evil; they had entered into death. And, because the result of sin is death, something or someone had to die to balance the account. Therefore, God by His own hands killed and skinned an innocent lamb in order to provide clothes for Adam and Eve. Through this act, God demonstrated to them and to us that true worship is acknowledging our sinfulness and His holiness through the offering of a blood sacrifice, a sacrifice of life for sin. And, because of the sin-death that had entered into the human race through Adam's act of disobedience, God's hand was forced and He closed the way to the tree of life in the midst of the Garden. The only access since that sorrowful day is gained through the Lord Jesus Christ, Who is the Door (John 10:9). He is the Way (John 14:6). His blood shed on Calvary is the only key to the tree of life that waits in the Garden of the New Jerusalem.

Blunder Into Blessing

Through the Big Blunder of transferring his allegiance from his Creator God to Satan, the first Adam brought plague upon the earth and pain to mankind. But Jesus, the last Adam, through His example of perfect obedience to the Father, offers reconciliation and eternal life. Christ can change the blunder into a blessing. He is the door to a garden far lovelier than the Garden of Eden. It is the garden of the New Jerusalem, the garden of holiness, peace and joy, where God will wipe away all tears and where there will be no death and no pain.

Christians have indeed gained more than Adam lost. He lost the passive state of innocence, but we gained the positive standing before God of the righteousness of His Son. We are candidates for jobs in eternity, when one shall rule over five cities, one shall rule over ten cities, and where everyone will have his own vine and fig tree (Luke 19:17; Micah 4:4).

At that time, the tempter, Satan, will be cast into the lake of fire, *"prepared for the devil and his angels"* (Matt. 25:41). There will be no place for him in the universe except hell. All that the devil accomplished through deception, Jesus can redeem. The Big Blunder can become the Big Blessing through Him. He can take care of it, and He can take care of any other problem that plagues the human race. He can take care of every problem in my life and every problem in your life.

The forces of alcoholism are broken by the power of His truth. The stranglehold of nicotine is crushed by the strength of His love.

The evil forces behind illicit love flee in the face of His glory. The bondage of a lying and cheating spirit is broken in His presence.

Did Adam ever repent? We don't know. We do know that, even though his first son was a murderer, he lived to see his great great great great grandson Enoch walk in intimate communion with God. But, even then, the whole world was so corrupt before God that only three generations after Enoch, God destroyed all living things by the Flood.

8

The Big Surprise

Ten Generations

God took the first chapter of Genesis to tell the story of creation. He took the second chapter to tell about the creation of man. He took the rest of the entire Bible to tell how He is working to bring man back to his ordained position of authority.

Adam was the first man.

Seth was his third son through whom the bloodline of the Promised Seed would continue.

Enos was Adam's grandson.

Cainan, Adam's great grandson.

Mahalaleel, his great great grandson.

Jared, his great great great grandson.

Enoch, the sixth from Adam, his great great great great grandson.

Methuselah, the seventh from Adam, lived 969 years, longer than any other man recorded in the Bible.

Lamech, the eighth from Adam.

Noah, the ninth from Adam.

Counting Adam, there are ten generations from Adam to Noah.

In the fifth chapter of Genesis, in the middle of a lengthy geneology of "he lived, he

begat, he died, he lived, he begat, he died,"
there is a Big Surprise.

"Enoch walked with God after he begat Methuselah three hundred years, and begat sons and daughters: And all the days of Enoch were three hundred sixty and five years: And Enoch walked with God: and he was not; for God took him" (5:22-24).

Genesis, with all its mighty miracles, its wonderful and dramatic revelations, had an astounding first, the experience of Enoch that points ahead to what God has planned for His Church.

"Enoch walked with God, and he was not, for God took him."

Enoch was caught away from earth to heaven without experiencing physical death.

As for Adam, as far as we know, he never again saw the face of God after he was banished from the Garden. From that time forth there appears no recorded communication between Adam and his Maker. There is, however, evidence in the records that the succeeding generations of Adam's sons and grandsons, perhaps filled with resentment over what had been lost to them through Adam's sin, turned farther and farther from God until the day God said, *"I repent that I made man"* (6:6,7).

A Light In The Darkness

But the black cloud had its silver lining. In

the darkness of the hour, when men were racing toward destruction, Enoch appeared, brightening the horizon and changing the order of the day. Enoch was a contemporary of Adam for 308 years, watching Adam's progeny in rebellion against God, live in sin and die in sin. But he broke the pattern by faith. He snapped the chain of sin and death.

"By faith Enoch was translated (changed from one place or condition or form to another [Scribner-Bantam English Dictionary]) *that he should not see death, and was not found, because God had translated him; for before his translation he had this testimony, that he pleased God"*(Heb. 11:5).

Search parties combed the area, but he was not found.

Search parties several generations later were sent to seek for the Prophet Elijah after he, too, was translated by God (see 2 Kings 2:11); neither was he found.

Today's atheists, scientists, evolutionists, humanists and skeptics are still searching for ways to disprove God's miracles, but He keeps right on doing what He has been doing all along. There is nothing new under the sun. It's all in the book of Genesis.

Enoch's testimony to the people of his day was his godly conduct and speech. He was no silent witness.

I don't want silent witnesses to take the

stand for me. I don't want anybody vouching for me by smiling and looking good. I want them to talk and tell what they know.

Enoch pleased God by talking about Him and telling about His goodness, about His love, about His provisions for man's redemption. He preached to the multitudes about sin and forgiveness. He did what God called him to do, and he pleased God. When he finished, instead of having to die, God took him home.

Enoch And Adam

Enoch had heard about God from his great great great great grandfather Adam. They probably took long walks together in the woods and had long talks about God and about the Garden of Eden.

"What is God like, Grandpa? How big is He? How tall is He?"

And Adam would say, "We used to walk with Him every evening in the cool of the day. From His loins downward He was dressed in fire and from His loins upward He was dressed in fire. I looked just like Him in those days. I didn't wear this old smelly coat of skins. I wore a cloak of light."

"You sure don't wear a cloak of light now, Grandpa! What happened? How did you and Grandma Eve lose the right to live in the Garden?"

"Well, Enoch, we mistreated God. We stole the fruit He had reserved for Himself.

We disobeyed Him, we rebelled against Him, and when something inside of us changed, we had to leave His presence. And we've never seen Him since."

"I want to see Him, Grandpa. How can I see Him?"

"He won't let you see Him. He won't let anybody see Him, you see, because now we're all sinners."

"But I'm not! I haven't done anything against God. I'm going to have a talk with Him. I'm going to find God and do whatever He tells me to do. If He walked with you, Grandpa, He'll walk with me."

So, young Enoch believed he could do anything that had been done before. "And Enoch walked with God," and he became a prophet.

"And Enoch, also, the seventh from Adam, prophesied of these, saying, Behold, the Lord cometh with ten thousands of his saints, To execute judgment upon all, and to convince all that are ungodly among them of all their ungodly deeds which they have ungodly committed, and of all their hard speeches which ungodly sinners have spoken against him" (Jude 14,15).

When a son was born into his family, Enoch prophesied to the world through the son's name that God had just about had enough. The son's name was Methuselah, which means, "At his death, judgment comes". Enoch believed in judgment. In the midst of gross sin, the quagmire, muck and mess of sin, he preached righteousness and judgment. And, even though the people kept on cultivating their evil imaginations, God in His mercy pushed back the day of judgment as long as possible and postponed Methuselah's death until he was 969 years old.

"The Lord is not slack concerning his promise, as some men count slackness; but is longsuffering to us-ward, not willing that any should perish, but that all should come to repentance" (2 Peter 3:9).

God did not want to judge the earth. He gave man plenty of time to repent and to seek Him. But sin had become a cancer, spreading in every direction, destroying people, destroying homes, and destroying the civilization. Infants were burned to death on the stone hands of idols; sodomy was rampant--men with men, men with animals; even men with statues. Temple prostitution was common. Drunkenness was the norm. But in the darkness of superstition and sin, persistent Enoch found God. God had not deserted man at all.

Enoch And God

When Enoch walked with God, he didn't have time to walk with sinners. That made him stand out; that made him peculiar; that made him strange. His neighbors believed only what they could see with their eyes. They could not see his invisible Companion, so they thought He wasn't there. Enoch was walking arm-in-arm with God, and the people thought he was crazy.

By the time Enoch was 365 years old, he and God were old friends. They had a lot to talk about. And, one day they walked a long long way, just talking.

Maybe Enoch said, "Well, God, I've got to be going back. My wife doesn't like my getting home late for dinner. I sure do thank You for my good wife. She's a good cook and a good woman."

Maybe God said, "My home is about as close as yours. Why don't you just come home with Me?"

"That's a very tempting invitation, God," Enoch might have said. "You never invited me to Your home before."

"I'm inviting you now."

"Will I ever come back?"

"No, Enoch, you won't come back."

"But, God, don't I have to die first? Everybody is supposed to die."

"Everybody but you. You've walked so faithfully with Me, I'm going to do something special for you. I'll take you right on home without dying first."

"What about my wife?"

"She'll be along soon to be with us forever. Let's go on home for your celebration."

God gave him a touch, and gravity loosed Enoch. He was changed *"in the twinkling of an eye"* (1 Cor. 15:52), and moved with God through the stellar regions. They went by the moon and it was a dry place. They passed Mars and there was nobody there. Up, up through the extragalactic nebulae they went together. Further and further from dimension to dimension they traveled.

Then Enoch said, "I see something so bright…"

"That's home."

"I hear singing. I hear music…"

"That's your welcome."

"Lift up your heads, O ye gates; even lift them up, ye everlasting doors; and the King of glory shall come in. Who is this King of glory? The Lord of hosts, he is the King of glory" (Psalm 24:9,10).

As they swept through the gates of pearl, the angels sang and shouted, "Welcome, Enoch! Welcome forever! You walked with God and He has brought you home!"

As a recompense for his humility, for his faithfulness, for his willingness to walk with God, for his burning desire to know God and to serve Him, Enoch "was not, for God took him."

It's For Us, Too!

The account of Enoch is the Old Testament foreshadowing of the future translation of God's saints, still living when He comes to take them out of the world. Neither will they experience the pains of physical death. They, too, will *"be changed, in a moment, in the twinkling of an eye."*

"Behold, I shew you a mystery; We shall not all sleep, but we shall all be changed, In a moment, in the twinkling of an eye, at the last trump: for the trumpet shall sound, and the dead shall be raised incorruptible, and we shall be changed... O death, where is thy sting? O grave, where is thy victory?" (1 Cor. 15:51,52,55)

"But I would not have you to be ignorant, brethren, concerning them which are asleep, that ye sorrow not, even as others which have no hope. For if we believe that Jesus died and rose again, even so them also which sleep in Jesus will God bring with him. For this we say unto you by the word of the Lord, that we which are alive and remain unto the coming of the Lord shall not prevent them which are asleep. For the Lord himself shall descend from heaven with a shout, with the voice of the archangel, and with the trump of God: and the dead in Christ shall rise first: Then we which are alive and remain shall be caught up together with them in the clouds, to meet the

Lord in the air: and so shall we ever be with the Lord. Wherefore comfort one another with these words" (1 Thess. 4:13-18).

Life in this world is a school to prepare the saints of God for life out of this world, eternal life during which man will again rule the universe with God. We are being equipped for eternity. We are practicing for eternity. One day soon it will be spoken of the Church as it is of Enoch: "She walked with God and is not, for God took her."

9

The Big Waters

In Touch

Genesis is neither remote from life today, nor are its stories dissociated one from another. It is a contemporary book. It has continuity. The events flow and the people are in touch.

Most people today are in touch with five generations. For example, I didn't know either of my great grandfathers at all, but I knew my Grandfather Sumrall very well, and I learned much about the Civil War through Grandpa Sumrall who wore his Civil War uniform every day for years and was finally buried in it. I also knew my father very well, and from him I learned about his day and times. I know myself, and I know my sons and grandsons. That's five generations.

Just ten generations connect Adam and Noah. During those ten generations, Methuselah was contemporary with both. Mankind was just one big happy, unhappy family.

"It came to pass, when men began to multiply on the face of the earth, and daughters were born unto them, That the sons of God saw the daughters of men that they

were fair; and they took them wives of all which they chose" (6:1,2).

The sons of Elohim in this passage are the same sons of Elohim appearing before God's throne in the book of Job, chapters 1 and 2. They comprise the original priesthood on the earth, the forerunners of Melchisedek, who:

"...without father, without mother, without descent, having neither beginning of days, nor end of life; but made like unto the Son of God; abideth a priest continually" (Heb. 7:3).

The sons of God, these members of the eternal priesthood, lusted after the daughters of red earth and married them. Their offspring were giants, evil ten-foot tall freaks with twelve fingers and twelve toes. It was Satan, seducing the whole earth into wholesale corruption in order to negate God's prophecy that the Seed of the Woman would destroy him. He was determined that there would be no holy Seed of the Woman. Therefore, he enticed the sons of Elohim to intermarry with the daughters of earth in order to contaminate all seed. Adam was right there to see all the monstrous results of his disobedience, while Satan flaunted in his face the fact that the devil could not be defeated by those who did the works of the devil.

"And the Lord said, My spirit shall not always strive with man, for that he also is

flesh... And God saw that the wickedness of man was great in the earth, and that every imagination of the thoughts of his heart was only evil continually... And the Lord said, I will destroy man whom I have created from the face of the earth; both man, and beast, and the creeping thing, and the fowls of the air; for it repenteth me that I have made them... yet his days shall be an hundred and twenty years" (6:3,5,7,3).

No One But Noah

God gave man 120 years to repent and to be reconciled with Him and with his fellow man. No one repented. No one desired to walk with God. No one believed. But Noah...

On the face of the whole planet earth, God found one righteous man to whom He could entrust the sacred bloodline.

"But Noah found grace in the eyes of the Lord. ... Noah was a just man, and perfect in his generations, and Noah walked with God... And God said unto Noah, The end of all flesh is come before me; for the earth is filled with violence through them; and behold, I will destroy them with the earth" (6:8,9,13).

The corruption of man, even the corruption of the earth itself, is not new. Lying and killing and destroying are not new. Drunkenness, sodomy and adultery, perjury and burglary are not new. The whole world groaned under it. Only one man kept himself separated from the rampant crime and idolatry, Noah. And because of his righteousness, his family was included in God's mercy.

"Make thee an ark of gopher wood; rooms shalt thou make in the ark... And this is the fashion which thou shalt make it of..." (vs. 14,15)

And God gave Noah detailed instructions to build and prepare the Ark of Safety for himself and for his family.

"And, behold, I, even I, do bring a flood of waters upon the earth, to destroy all flesh... But with thee will I establish my covenant; and thou shalt come into the ark, thou, and thy sons, and thy wife, and thy sons' wives with thee. And of every living thing of all flesh... And take thou unto thee of all food that is eaten... Thus did Noah; according to all that God commanded him, so did he" (6:17-19,21,22).

According to detailed instructions, Noah built the ark, a three-story, watertight, seaworthy vessel, 450' by 75' by 45', with a long narrow window across the top and one door set in the side.

Disclaimers Of The Word

Church pulpiteers have for centuries challenged and attempted to discredit God's Word concerning Noah's ark. For centuries until 1850 no man could believe that a boat that large would float. But someday God will unearth the ark on Mount Ararat in Armenia, where the Bible records that it landed. Man will again walk into the ark, touch the walls, examine the structure and applaud the design, thereby certifying that the Bible is true, demonstrating that judgment is sure, and urging man to get right with God before it is too late.

For years the same pulpiteers claimed that the prophet Isaiah prophesied that Messiah would be born of a young woman, possibly married, not necessarily a virgin. Then God led men to some early manuscripts of Isaiah among the Dead Sea Scrolls. These ancient copies specifically designate an unmarried virgin to give birth to the Christ of God. The disclaimers of the virgin birth are now silent, as they will soon be about the ark.

For 120 years Noah prophesied the great Flood. Hired men helped him build the ark, receiving the wages of the day. They hauled timber, carved joints, whittled pegs, and mixed bitumen pitch for waterproofing, while they mocked Noah's warning of impending judgment. They gathered food and loaded the boat, but they ridiculed Noah's righteousness and his message. They admired his steadfastness and heard his prayers while they took his money, but their hearts were hardened by sin. Even today, many unsaved people help build churches, support charities, give money to the poor and help old ladies cross the street. Some of them who are actually teaching Sunday school have hearts caught in the snare of the world. Like Noah's neighbors, they are dangerously outside the Ark of Safety.

For 120 years Noah pleaded with the people, warning them of torrential rains where it had never rained before. Since the days of creation, the waters of heaven were contained in the firmament, filtering deadly space rays and making it possible for a man to live almost a thousand years. But on the day when Noah and his family stepped inside the ark and God locked the door behind them, the oceans convulsed and the heavens opened, and God purged the earth with a deluge from sky and sea. Unleashed rivers swirled over their banks. Oceans sent towering tidal waves crashing across the dry land. Maelstroms and hurricanes swept the earth, uprooting forests, slamming boulders into hillsides and mountains and crushing all living things in upon themselves--a catastrophic climax to the antideluvian world.

"All flesh died" (7:21).

All except Noah. He and his family bridged the gulf between the two worlds, the antideluvian and the post-deluvian.

God's Promise

For one full solar year Noah and his family ate, slept, prayed, tended the animals and cared for each other inside the ark. And they waited on God.

"And God spake unto Noah, saying, Go forth of the ark, thou, and thy wife, and thy sons, and thy sons' wives with thee. Bring forth with thee every living thing that is with thee...and be fruitful, and multiply upon the earth" (8:15-17).

"And Noah went forth...and builded an altar unto the Lord... And the Lord said in his heart, I will not again curse the ground any more for man's sake..." (8:18,20,21).

"And God blessed Noah and his sons... And God spake unto Noah and to his sons with him, saying, And I, behold, I establish my covenant with you, and with your seed after you...neither shall all flesh be cut off any more by the waters of a flood... This is the token of the covenant... I do set my bow in the cloud" (9:1,8,9,11-13).

God told Noah that He was breaking His covenant with Adam in favor of a new covenant with Noah, with his family and with every living creature that came off the ark. The token of that covenant was to be the rainbow, which man sees from one side and God sees from the other. The burden of the covenant was upon God Who promised never to destroy the earth again by water.

Since that time, perhaps because of the loss of the firmament filter, the average age of man has diminished from 900 to 120 to 70.

Sometimes the waters break loose in certain places to remind us what a great flood can do. But God's promise remains sure.

10

The Big Tower

Results Of Sin

The language of Adam and Eve continued from one generation to the next, from the Dispensation of Innocence through the Age of Conscience to Noah, then beyond the Flood to Noah's sons and grandsons into the Dispensation of Human Government. It was an age when God established the authority of civil government in which man is no longer solely answerable to God for his conduct, but also to man.

Noah begat Ham and Ham begat Cush and Cush begat Nimrod.

Because of Ham's wickedness, possibly a homosexual act (see Gen. 9:20-22), Noah prophesied against Ham's descendants and the curse fell upon Nimrod *"who began to be a mighty one in the earth...and the beginning of his kingdom was Babel".*(Babylon) (10:8,10).

"And it came to pass, as they journeyed from the east (from Ararat), *that they found a plain in the land of Shinar; and they dwelt there"* (11:2).

As they traveled to Shinar, a garden-like area between the Tigris and Euphrates Rivers,

Satan traveled with them, tempting them with the same Humanism with which he had successfully tempted Adam and Eve.

Satan is the number one promoter of Humanism, convincing man that he doesn't need God, that he can take care of himself. Because of Humanism, Adam and Eve were banished from the Garden of Eden. Because of Humanism, the anti-deluvian society was annihilated. Because of Humanism, the Moabite, Ammonite, Babylonian and Roman empires have crumbled. The devil destroys nations, he destroys civilizations, he destroys families, and he uses Humanism, self-exaltation.

Lucifer-Satan is a victim of his own folly. Maybe in heaven they call it "angelism". He wanted to make himself great. He wanted a name like Lucifer the Great, der Fuehrer Lucifer, or Generallissimo Lucifer, and because of his example, a third of the angels of heaven were cast down (2 Pet. 2:4). Millions die because others follow the wrong leader.

Gondwanaland Lost

During the time of Nimrod, the known world was one massive continent called Gondwanaland, encircled by the mighty seas. God had already told the people to scatter to the ends of it, to multiply and replenish the earth, but they decided to stick together and follow their leader Nimrod, worship the stars and climb to heaven their own way.

"And they said, Go to, let us build us a city and a tower, whose top may reach unto heaven; and let us make us a name, lest we be scattered abroad upon the face of the whole earth" (11:4).

Satan was right there, cheering them on. "Build it! Build it! Build your own Bab-el, your own 'Gate of God'!"

"And the Lord said, Behold, the people is one, and they have all one language; and this they begin to do: and now nothing will be restrained from them, which they have imagined to do " (11:6).

Nothing? Is God saying that men in unity can do anything they determine to do? Apparently so.

Jesus told His disciples: *"...if two of you shall agree on earth as touching any thing that they shall ask, it shall be done for them of my Father which is in heaven"* (Matt. 18:19).

The entire nation under Nimrod, sweating and swearing, firing bricks and hauling mortar to build the tower, were in agreement not to follow God but to follow their leader. The terraced pyramid became an enormous ediface, several city blocks square at the base, like a city of stone. Just three generations down the line from Noah and the Flood, sin-prone man decided to found his own religion, build his own "ark of safety," establish his own righteousness, and pave his way to heaven with his own hands.

"Yah, Jehovah!" they cried. "We don't need You! We don't believe in You! We have our own god! We are masters of our fate! We'll build our own escape from adversity! The tower! The tower! Bab-el! Bab-el!''

And the Lord said, *"Go to, let us go down, and there confound their language, that they may not understand one another's speech. So the Lord scattered them abroad from thence upon the face of all the earth: and they left off to build the city. Therefore is the name of it called Babel..."* (11:7-9).

Confusion

Bab-el, the "Gate of God," became Babel, "confusion" and babbling. *"God is not the author of confusion"* (1 Cor. 14:33); Humanism is the author of confusion.

If I greeted you with, "Good morning! How are you today?" you would smile and feel good and answer me. But if I said to you, "Wha'wah, wha'wah, wha'wah!" you would not answer me. You would think I was foolish. But, if you understood the Lisu tribal tongue, you would smile and answer. I had just said, "Peace to you. Peace to you. Divine peace to you."

So, God brought division and suspicion among the people in their rebellion by confounding them with over 2,000 diverse languages. One day they all spoke the same tongue; the next morning only the members of each clan could communicate. That causes trouble. That causes war.

Ham's brother Shem begat Arphaxad and

Arphaxad begat Eber and Eber begat Peleg.

The fourth generation from Noah through Shem was Peleg, whose name means "division". The earth's mass was still one at this time, but *"in his days was the earth divided"* (10:25). As God scattered the people, He also wrenched the continents apart with a mighty earthquake. We can see on a globe of the world how perfectly the continental coastlines correspond with one another. They will come back together in the Kingdom Age, at which time, the Bible tells us, *"there will be no more sea"* (Rev. 21:1).

God divided the mass of terra firma into continents, islands, archipelagoes and peninsulas in order to further separate man, that He might protect the bloodline of the Promised Seed from concentrated evil. He knew that men together who don't love God create evil, and that the big cities were citadels of sin and violence, sorrow and tears, heartaches and loneliness.

Sin draws man together from around the world to places like Las Vegas and Monte Carlo. Smiling orientals, aloof African princes, jet-setters, black aristocracy and white paupers, all colors and all languages, crowd the same gambling tables. But, language barriers separate. Welchmen have resisted their English neighbors for centuries in order to maintain the purity of the Welch language. The same is true of Scotland; the same, of Ireland. Their love of language reverts to the Tower of Babel. God's purpose there was to turn man's attention to Himself, but Satan persuaded the people to regard language as a matter of pride.

Many people have isolated themselves in jungles and deep mountain recesses, not because of skin color or body size, but because of language. In Central and South America and in Mexico, the ancient Indian civilizations are similar to that of ancient Egypt because their ancestors were together in Gondwanaland.

What is the answer? A miracle is happening all over the world, as the Holy Spirit of God blesses His people with the supernatural gift of tongues. World evangelists report that Christian charismatic congregations in Tokyo, Jerusalem, Johannesburg and Calcutta spontaneously sing in the spirit (1 Cor. 14:15) identical melodies and words, with identical accents and inflections, as their counterparts in London and Podunk. This phenomenon is but the forerunner of that great day when the curse is lifted from the earth, when Jesus Christ returns to set up His Kingdom in which the whole world will once again be of one language and one speech. Believing Jews expect this language to be pure melodic Hebrew.

11

The Big Man

A Heart For God

The continents were divided and the nations scattered. The people multiplied and replenished the earth as God had commanded, while God pursued His promise of the Savior, Who was to come from the woman Eve through a line of chief history makers-- through Seth, Enoch, Noah, Shem, Arphaxad, Eber and Peleg.

Genesis does not resound with echoes; it rings with voices. That's what the world needs today--strong voices for the glory of God.

In the country of the Chaldeans, in the city of Ur, a city given over to idolatry and demon worship, God found a man who was not an echo of other men but a voice strong for faith. He was Abram, the son of Terah, the son of Nahor, the son of Serug, the son of Reu, the son of Peleg; five generations from the time when the earth was divided, ten generations from Noah.

"Now the Lord had said unto Abram, Get thee out of thy country, and from thy kindred, and from thy father's house, unto a land that I will shew thee...By faith Abraham, when he was called to go out into a place

which he should after receive for an inheritance, obeyed; and he went out, not knowing whither he went" (12:1; Heb. 11:8).

The secret of the power of Abram is not mental capacity nor physical strength, but faith. He believed God spoke to him. He believed God spoke only truth. He believed that God could be trusted and that He was *"a rewarder of them that diligently seek him"* (Heb. 11:6).

Adam, the head of the human family.

Enoch, the Old Testament type of the New Testament Church.

Abraham, the big man of faith. Because of his great convictions, he was called on by God to make great decisions.

Other men found it easy to steal, to kill, to make an alabaster idol and call it god, to lie for gain, and to take another man's wife. These things were in their hearts. But in Abram's heart was faith to serve the one true and living God, Jehovah.

About 500 years after the Flood, God called Abram from Ur at the junction of the Tigris and Euphrates Rivers, the center of civilization and the future home of the Assyrians, Babylonians and Persians.

"And I will make of thee a great nation, and I will bless thee, and make thy name great; and thou shalt be a blessing: And I will bless them that bless thee, and curse him that

curseth thee: and in thee shall all families of the earth be blessed. So Abram departed, as the Lord had spoken unto him" (12:2-4).

Abram and his company traveled north along the Euphrates River, across the desert into Canaan, to a place of about 8,000 square miles known today as Israel, the Holy Land. It was an odyssey, a pilgrimage. He did not know where he was going; he was merely obeying God.

In the land of Canaan, *"Abram was very rich in cattle, in silver, and in gold"* (13:2). Serving Jehovah, the God with Whom Adam walked in the Garden, the God Whom Enoch served with all his heart, the God Whom Noah obeyed, did not make a poor man of Abram. He was a good man and a good businessman, and poverty was not the result of his obedience. God blessed him and changed his name from Abram, which means "exalted father," to Abraham, "father of nations."

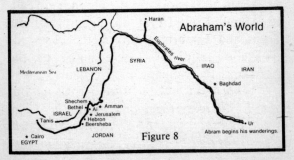

Figure 8

History's Most Popular Man

The prophetic nature of his name is true. Abraham is history's most popular man by multiplied millions. The Lord Jesus Christ is, of course, the greatest man who ever walked the earth, but Abraham is more popular even than Jesus. He is the father of the Jews and the father of the Arabs. He is also the father of every believer in Jesus Christ. (Gal. 3:7)

Men of great moral and spiritual strength emerge from the pages of Genesis in situations and places which did not seem ready for them. They appear to be before their time. But God's timing is perfect. In His plan, they were exactly on time. They were called by Him to be time-changers, spiritual and social world-changers, not in step with the world, but with God's own time-table.

Abraham was such a man. When the profile of a man towers into the sky, we need to study what kind of man he was, a man of faith and a man of decision.

There came a day when God decided to demonstrate to Abraham the extent of his faith. No doubt God already knew.

"And he said, Take now thy son, thine only son Isaac, whom thou lovest, and get thee into the land of Moriah; and offer him there for a burnt offering upon one of the mountains which I will tell thee of. And Abraham rose up early...and took...Isaac his

son...and went unto the place of which God had told him...and Abraham built an altar there...and took the knife to slay his son. And the angel of the Lord called unto him...Lay not thine hand upon the lad...for now I know that thou fearest God, seeing thou hast not withheld thy son...from me" (22:2,3,9-12).

"By faith...he that had received the promises offered up his only begotten son, Of whom it was said, That in Isaac shall thy seed be called" (Heb. 11:17,18).

In order to prove to God that he loved Him supremely above all else, Abraham took his precious son to the mountain at Jerusalem and prepared to sacrifice him on the altar.

By his actions he was saying to Isaac, "My beloved son, I have such faith in Jehovah Who gave you to me that, if you die here, God will raise you from the ashes, the same you with the same eyes, the same smile and the same love. I know that I will be taking you home with me back to your mother."

Abraham raised the knife to plunge it into his son's heart, but the angel of the Lord intervened.

"Hold on, Abraham, " he shouted. "Here is the sacrifice, this ram caught in the bush. He is the substitute."

Abraham looked up at the raised knife, glinting in the sunlight. He lowered it and with it cut the cords binding Isaac on the altar. With the same knife he killed the ram and burned it as a sacrifice to God.

The Vision

As the smoke rose to heaven, God said to Abraham, "Look."

He looked. A few hundred yards to the north on a hill without walls, without buildings, he saw Mount Calvary.

"What is it, Lord? What is happening there? Nobody ever hung like that before on a cross of wood. What does it mean?"

And God answered. "That is My Son. You have pleased Me, so you may take your son home. But I will sacrifice My Son Who will be the salvation of the world."

"I see it, Lord," said Abraham, as he bowed his face to the ground. "Yes, Lord, I see it now."

"Abraham rejoiced to see my day," Jesus said, *"and he saw it and was glad"* (John 8:56).

For the rest of his life, from that memorial day on Mount Moriah, Abraham continually *"looked for a city* (the New Jerusalem)... *whose builder and maker is God"* (Heb. 11:10).

12

The Big Promotion

Eleventh Son

Abraham, through Isaac and Isaac's son Jacob, became the father of the Jewish nation. Jacob, whom God renamed Israel, had two wives: Leah, the older, and Rachel, the favorite. Leah and Rachel's servant-girls, Bilhah and Zilpah, became Jacob's concubines. Through these four women, Jacob fathered twelve sons, who in turn became the fathers of the twelve tribes of Israel.

Leah first bare four sons: Reuben, Simeon, Levi and Judah. Bilhah, Rachel's maid, then gave birth to Dan and Naphtali. She was followed by Zilpah, Leah's maid, who had Gad and Asher. Leah bare two more sons, Issachar and Zebulun, before she gave Jacob his only daughter, Dinah. Finally, Rachel conceived and gave birth to Joseph and, much later, Benjamin.

Joseph, the eleventh son, came to history from a big family destined to become a group of consolidated tribes, and ultimately a nation that would alter the course of world history.

The Coat Of Human Affection

Youngest sons are often pampered, and

Joseph was no exception. Because his mother Rachel was the favorite wife, his father Jacob preferred him above the others. While his older brothers were obliged to tend the herds of cattle and sheep in the fields and hills, they came to resent their father's lavish love for the favored son and to hate Joseph himself. And, when Jacob unwisely presented Joseph with a luxurious coat of many colors far more elegant than the robes and skins his brothers wore, he fanned the jealousy. The coat of many colors was a Coat of Human Affection, and the ten sons of Leah, Bilhah and Zilpah burned with indignation. They were already angry with Joseph for reporting their sinful conduct, their robberies and murders and adulteries while away from home, to their father. But when young Joseph told them a dream he had, they were infuriated.

"...Joseph, being seventeen years old...dreamed a dream, and he told it his brethren: and they hated him yet the more. And he said unto them, Hear, I pray you, this dream... For, behold, we were binding sheaves in the field, and, lo, my sheaf arose, and also stood upright; and, behold, your sheaves stood round about, and made obeisance to my sheaf" (37:2,5-7).

"What is that supposed to mean?" they said. "That you're going to have dominion over us? That we're going to bow down to you? That's a laugh!"

"And he dreamed yet another dream, and told it his brethren, and said, Behold, I have dreamed a dream more; and, behold, the sun and the moon and the eleven stars made obeisance to me" (37:9).

This time his father too rebuked him. "Does that mean that not only your brothers, but your mother and I also, will bow down to you?"

But Jacob was not really angry with Joseph. He continued to treat him as the family favorite. The Coat of Human Affection was still his badge of priority, but one day it got him into trouble.

Joseph was sent to the fields to check on his brothers.

"Here comes that dreamer!" they murmured among themselves, and they plotted to kill him, dip his fancy coat in blood and send it back to their father, blaming his death on some wild animal.

Reuben overruled. So, after yanking the coat off his back, the brothers threw Joseph into a dry waterhole to keep him prisoner until they decided what to do with him. Later, during Reuben's absence, they pulled him out of the pit and sold him as a slave to some passing Ishmaelite cousins from Midian, who were traveling to Egypt. Whether Joseph was unconscious or awake and resisting, the Bible doesn't say. It does say that, after a dream of greatness and power and authority, Joseph became a slave in a foreign land, a servant to Potipher, Pharaoh's captain of the guard. His first coat, the Coat of Human Affection, had let him down.

Joseph lost no time moaning and groaning and day-dreaming about the past. He got busy. He learned the language and the customs. He learned his job and he worked hard.

The Coat Of Human Authority

Joseph was soon promoted to the position of top man in the rich man's house, where he received his second coat, the Coat of Human Authority. He conducted Potipher's business. He managed the finances, supervised the servants, governed the household, and saw to it that everything was clean and in good repair. He was loyal to Potipher and faithful to the God of his fathers, while growing in wisdom, strength and beauty.

Potipher's wife was watching him. She hated him because he was ethical, moral and virtuous, while she, though beautiful, was a licentious woman, filled with lust. She wanted to break him and make him carnal like herself.

"Someday somehow I'm going to get that Hebrew in bed with me," she promised herself. And, whenever her husband was away

from the house, she would try to entice him.
But Joseph would not respond.

Day after day she pressed him. Finally, in
a fit of anger, she clutched his robe, the Coat
of Human Authority, and would not let go.
She would prove to him who had authority in
that house! But Joseph, rather than com-
promise, left the coat with her and fled.

Whether or not Potipher believed her lies,
that Joseph had tried to seduce her, he
sentenced Joseph to an indeterminate
sentence in prison.

The short-lived Coat of Human Affection
is not greatness.

The short-lived Coat of Human Authority
is not greatness.

Promotion by man is temporal, and is not
greatness.

When our Great God advances a man,
that is greatness. God lifts up and God casts
down. God can put us in office when nobody
else can. God can prosper us when others are
not being prospered. God humbles us for His
own purposes, and exalts us when it's time.

Joseph lost coat number two. He lost coat
number one because he dreamed a dream
before he learned the value of tact. He lost
coat number two because of a lustful woman.
But when Joseph arrived in chains at the
prison, he was singing an archaic Hebrew version of "That Old Time Religion, It's Good

Enough For Me!'' He remembered the dreams, and he knew God was faithful.

In the prison he went to work. Never was an Egyptian dungeon as clean as that one when Joseph got through with it. Nothing in Egypt was that clean, not even Pharaoh's palace. He killed the rats. He killed the roaches. He cleaned the commodes. He cleaned the urinals. He cleaned the scullery.

The warden said, ''My, oh my, I don't know why that young man is here, but I've never had it so good. Is he ever a worker! He gets up before dawn and, after praying to his God, he rouses those lazy Egyptians. He puts them to work and gets them singing about some old-time religion. He tells them about some dreams he had, and they all laugh at him because here he is, a prisoner in this place. But he laughs, too, then sends them back to work. This is the cleanest place in the empire. We have no fights, we have no insurrection, and that one man is the reason. The remarkable thing about him is that nobody tells him to do anything. He just does it.'' And he put Joseph in charge of the prison.

The Robe Of Divine Revelation

During the ten years that Joseph ran the prison, behind the scenes God was working.

When Joseph was thirty years old, Pharaoh dreamed a dream, a wild dream about seven ears of healthy corn being eaten by seven ears of withered corn. Now, corn doesn't eat corn! He dreamed about seven fat cows being eaten by seven lean cows. Cows don't eat cows! He told the dream to the court magicians and soothsayers, and demanded from them the interpretation. They had nothing to say. They couldn't even make up anything. But Pharaoh's butler remembered that, when he himself was in prison, a man named Joseph interpreted dreams for the prisoners, and they all came true just like he said.

"Send for that man!" Pharaoh demanded.

Immediately, a courier on horseback was dispatched to the prison.

"The man named Joseph," he shouted breathlessly, "is he here?"

"Sure, he's here," the warden said. "He's our number one prisoner. Why do you want him?"

"Pharaoh summons him to the royal presence."

"Come on, now! What would the king want with a foreign prisoner?"

"Send him immediately! Pharaoh is waiting!"

...and they brought him hastily out of the dungeon; and he shaved himself, and changed his raiment...

(The third coat, the spiritual Robe of

Divine Revelation, was placed upon Joseph by God Himself.)

"...and (he) *came in unto Pharaoh. And Pharaoh said unto Joseph, I have dreamed a dream, and there is none that can interpret it: and I have heard say of thee, that thou canst understand a dream to interpret it. And Joseph answered Pharaoh, saying, It is not in me: God shall give Pharaoh an answer of peace"* (41:14-16).

So Pharaoh told Joseph his dream, and Joseph gave the interpretation as God showed it to him.

The seven healthy ears of corn and the seven fat cows represented seven years of a plenteous harvest. The seven withered ears of corn and the seven lean cows represented seven years of drought and famine.

Then Joseph said, *"Now therefore let Pharaoh look out a man discreet and wise, and set him over the land of Egypt...and let him appoint officers over the land, and take up the fifth part of the land of Egypt in the seven plenteous years... And that food shall be for store to the land against the seven years of famine... And Pharaoh said unto Joseph, Forasmuch as God hath shewed thee all this...See, I have set thee over all the land of Egypt"* (41:33,34,36,39,41).

Pharaoh then gave Joseph the ring from his finger, clothed him in a linen vesture and put a gold chain around his neck--royal acknowledgement of the Robe of Divine Revelation. Joseph wore that coat until he died. Nobody could take it away from him. It was the mantle of the King.

Joseph's Revenge

Did Joseph take revenge upon Potipher's wife? No.

Did Joseph take revenge upon his brothers?

After two years of famine, when the storehouses of the world were empty and the storehouses of Egypt were still full, ten men crawled on hands and knees with their faces to the floor, down the magnificent thick purple carpet before Joseph's throne. They were Reuben, Simeon, Levi, Judah, Dan, Naphtali, Gad, Asher, Issachar and Zebulon. Joseph, closing his eyes, envisioned his 23-year-old dream--ten sheaves bowing before his sheaf. The brothers had come for corn. Overcome with emotion, Joseph sent them back home to bring the youngest brother, Benjamin, Rachel's second son, back with them to Egypt. Upon their return with Benjamin, he revealed himself to them.

"You meant it for evil," he said, "but God meant it for good." Then he raised them to their feet, put his arms around their necks, and wept.

"How is our father?" he asked them. "Is

it well with him? I've missed you.''

Because Joseph was a great man of God, he summoned the entire clan of starving Israelites to Egypt, to the lush land of Goshen in the Nile delta. There he preserved them and kept them in safety, God's man preserving the Promised Seed, until God would send the Deliverer.

EPILOGUE

Both Scripture and tradition attribute the authorship of Genesis to Moses. The first eleven chapters tell the story of man from creation to the beginning of the life of Abraham. Genesis chapters 12 through 50 recount Jehovah's dealings with Abraham, Isaac and Jacob and their descendants. The rest of the Bible shows how God, through these people, revealed His nature and His ways to the world, to establish His will and bring redemption to all men.

Each of the great men in Genesis typifies the Christ Who was to come:

Adam, the first of his kind, whose father is God;

Abel, the true sacrifice;

Enoch, the caught-away one;

Noah, the faithful prophet;

Abraham, who walked by faith;

Isaac, the peace-giver;

Jacob, the prince of Israel; and

Joseph, the sustainer of life. (See Appendix, "Joseph, a Type of Christ, 30 Ways," page 123.)

Genesis, like Malachi, the final book in the Hebrew Bible, closes with silence, 430 years of silence from God. (Ex. 12:40) But the narrative continues and the revelation of God progresses as though the break had been but a day, God remembering His people.

"How can I find the Way?"

"Where among the library stacks is Truth?"

"What is the purpose of Life?"

The Lord Jesus Christ said of Himself, "I AM."

"I am the way, the truth, and the life: no man cometh unto the Father, but by me" (John 14:6).

Appendix
Joseph, A Type Of Christ
30 Ways

JOSEPH   JESUS

1. Loved by his father.   "This is my beloved
   Gen. 37:3   Son" (Matt. 3:17).

2. Hated by his   "...they...hated both
   brothers. Gen. 37:4   me and my father"
                               (John 15:24b).

3. Brothers did not be-   "...neither did his
   lieve him. Gen. 37:8   brethren believe him"
                               (John 7:5).

4. Brothers rejected his   "We will not have
   reign. Gen. 37:20   this man to reign over
                               us" (Luke 19:14b).

5. Brothers conspired   "...took counsel
   against him.   against Jesus to put
   Gen. 37:18   him to death" (Matt.
                               27:1).

6. Mocked. Gen. 37:19   "...after that they had
                               mocked him..."
                               (Matt. 27:31).

7. Stripped of his coat.   "...and they stripped
   Gen. 37.23   him" (Matt. 27:28a).

8. Sold for silver. Gen. 37:28

"...and they (sold Him) for thirty pieces of silver" (Matt. 26:15).

9. All that he did, prospered in his hand. Gen. 39:3

"...the pleasure of the Lord shall prosper in his hand" (Isa. 53:10c).

10. All things were put into his hand. Gen. 39:4-8

"The Father...hath given all things into his hand" (John 3:35).

11. Tempted, but did not sin. Gen. 39:9

"...tempted as we are ...yet without sin" (Heb. 4:15).

12. Bound and imprisoned... Gen. 39:20

"...bound him and they led him away" (Matt. 27:2).

13. ...with two malefactors. Gen. 40:2

"And there were also two other, malefactors,...with him" (Luke 23:32).

14. One received the message of life, but the other died. Gen. 40:21,22

"Today shalt thou be with me in paradise" (Luke 23:43b).

15. None so discreet and wise. Gen. 41:39

"In whom are hid all the treasures of wisdom and knowledge" (Col. 2:3).

16. They bowed the knee to him. Gen. 41:43

"...every knee shall bow..." (Phil. 2:10).

17. Thirty years old when service began. Gen. 41:46

"Thirty years old when ministry began" (Luke 3:23 NS).

18. God used his suffering to save others. Gen. 50:20

"God used Christ's suffering to bring salvation" (Rom. 5:8 NS).

19. Given power over all Egypt. Gen. 41:41

"All power is given unto me..." (Matt. 28:18).

20. Gentile bride to share his glory. Gen. 41:45

"Bride of Christ to share his glory forever" (John 14:1-3 NS).

21. God promised him a place of authority. Gen. 37:6,7

"...the government shall be upon his shoulders" (Isa. 9:6).

22. Cast into a pit, but delivered out of it. Gen. 37:24,28

"Now he that ascended, what is it but that he also descended first into the lower parts of the earth?" (Eph. 4:9).

23. Imprisoned on false charges. Gen. 39:17-20

"...for many bear false witness against him" (Mark 14:56).

24. His dealings with his brothers brought them to repentance. Gen. 50:18

"I have heard of thee with the hearing of the ears, but now my eye seeth thee; Wherefore, I abhor myself and repent in dust and ashes" (Job 42:5,6).

25. Joseph revealed himself to his brothers during their imprisonment. Gen. 45:1

"...by which he preached to the spirits in prison" (2 Pet. 3:19).

26. Taken to Egypt by somebody else. Gen. 37:28

"...he took the young child and his mother by night, and departed into Egypt" (Matt. 2:14).

27. Joseph wept. Gen. 42:24

"Jesus wept" (John 11:35).

28. He had compassion. Gen. 45:5

"He was moved with compassion" (Matt. 9:36).

29. Told them not to fear. Gen. 50:19

"Told his disciples not to fear" (Luke 12:32).

30. Forgave them and reinstated them to position of authority. Gen. 50:21

"Forgave them and reinstated them to position of authority" (Luke 24:47,49 NS).